Alexander Taylor Innes

Studies in Scottish history

Chiefly ecclesiastical

Alexander Taylor Innes

Studies in Scottish history
Chiefly ecclesiastical

ISBN/EAN: 9783337233310

Printed in Europe, USA, Canada, Australia, Japan

Cover: Foto ©ninafisch / pixelio.de

More available books at **www.hansebooks.com**

STUDIES

IN

SCOTTISH HISTORY

CHIEFLY ECCLESIASTICAL

BY

A. TAYLOR INNES

ADVOCATE

AUTHOR OF "THE LAW OF CREEDS IN SCOTLAND," AND "CHURCH
AND STATE: A HISTORICAL MANUAL"

London

HODDER AND STOUGHTON

27, PATERNOSTER ROW

MDCCCXCII

Printed by Hasell, Watson, & Viney, Ld., London and Aylesbury.

PREFACE.

THE two opening essays are biographical.
They treat, I think for the first time, of
paradoxes in character which happen also to
illustrate a great problem in history. Most of
the others deal with that historical problem
in its later forms. For it is still unsolved—
at least on the side of practice. Yet no one
has gone more than a few inches below
the surface of our Northern annals without
striking upon it. And ever since, half a
century ago, it broke out in unexpected disruption, it has been to intelligent men
elsewhere a subject of curious inquiry, while
to those within Scotland it has become—

never more than in the present year—a question of conscience and of duty.

I have to express my thanks to the following publishers, Messrs. Isbister & Co., Messrs. W. Blackwood & Sons, Messrs. Hodder & Stoughton, Messrs. T. Nelson & Sons, and Messrs. Macniven & Wallace, for permission to include in this series some papers and fragments which have already appeared in print.

EDINBURGH, *April* 1892.

CONTENTS.

I.

SAMUEL RUTHERFURD.

SAMUEL RUTHERFURD.

WHEN you explore an island, it is sometimes an advantage to step ashore at a point opposite to that at which previous voyagers have landed. Most men who know Samuel Rutherfurd at all know him as the author of *Rutherfurd's Letters.* When I knew him first, I knew him as the author of *Lex Rex.*

Lex Rex is one of the few important books on constitutional law which Scotland has produced. Bearing the sub-title of *A Dispute for the Just Prerogative of King and People*, it is really a discussion of the then pressing question of absolutism. " Whether the King be above the Law, or no," involved in those days the practical questions whether he could modify the law and dispense with its exercise on the one hand, and whether the people, on the other hand, could resist him in defence of it. To solve these questions Rutherfurd had to go to the foundations of politics. Government in general, he lays it down,

3

is from God, and is by His authority. But the
particular form of government is by the voluntary
choice of men ; and "the aptitude and temper of
every commonwealth to monarchy rather than to
democracy or aristocracy, is God's warrant and
call to determine the wills and liberty of the
people to pitch upon a monarchy, *hic et nunc*,
rather than any other form of government,
though all the three be from God." It follows
that there remains a certain sovereignty in the
people, and a right to modify or limit, and, in
case of necessity, to recall the power already
given, while that power must, of course, be always
kept within the law. The right of the king is
therefore a fiduciary right : he is trustee for the
people whom God, by their own choice, has com-
mitted to him. And he is in trust in order to
administer the law, not to break it, nor to dispense with it, nor yet to enforce his private interpretation of it. Interpretation is the business of
his judges, and judges are *ministri regni, non
regis :* they are not his private servants, but his
public officers, responsible directly to God for
administration of the law according to their consciences, not according to his. The king is thus
the highest official, and absolute power is contrary
to nature, irrational, and unlawful. The people

have indeed no right to give up their liberties irrevocably, whether it be to Parliament or to king, to one man or to many. Much of this doctrine has become the constitutional inheritance of all countries in modern times. But in that age the author narrowly escaped, and the book itself did not escape, the hands of the common hangman. Yet its theories were the same which in the previous century had illustrated Scotland in the famous book of George Buchanan, and which were continued through the generation after Rutherfurd by the *Informatory Vindication*, the *Jus Populi*, and other manifestoes of the Covenanters, down to that Revolution of 1688 which gave so great a part of them an historical embodiment. But Rutherfurd's treatise is much longer, and also more learned and more logical than the others; and as we hew our way through the forty-four stiff chapters of *Lex Rex*, where the rights of man are so strangely intertwisted with feudal royalism on the one hand, and covenanting religion on the other, it is hard to believe that all this was the work of the same author who carelessly flung out upon his age what we still recognise as the most seraphic book in our literature.

What then was the life of the man who embraced in his life two such extremes?

Rutherfurd [1] was born about A.D. 1600, and his years thus run parallel with the first sixty of that century. From Jedburgh, or its neighbourhood, he came as a student to the College of Edinburgh in 1617. Four years thereafter he passed as Master of Arts, and two years later, in 1623, he was elected Professor of Humanity in his University. Up to this time his studies seem to have chiefly been in the region of classics and philosophy, including logic according to the system of Ramus. But in 1625, on account of an accusation of immorality which has never been cleared up,[2] he demitted his chair in the University. What he did during the next two years is not known in detail, but he seems now to have betaken himself more to the refuge of religion, as

[1] So he uniformly spells his own name on his many title-pages from 1643 to 1659. The fact that in earlier years he had sometimes written his name Rutherfoord, and also Rutherfuird (never, so far as I have yet seen, Rutherford), shows that he was aware of a possible variety of spelling, and deliberately chose that form which his life-long adoption (down even to his "Latter Will" in 1661) makes binding upon us. In his Latin books the author's name is quaintly given as *Rhaetorfortis* (1636), or *Retorfortis* (1651).

[2] There are some puzzling points in this part of the history. It is very fairly stated in Murray's *Life of Rutherford* : Edinburgh, 1827.

he certainly did to the engrossing study of
theology. Only two years later, at all events, we
find him settled as minister at Anwoth, and devoting himself to the work of the pastorate there
with a zeal which even he afterwards looked back
upon with envy. Rising at three in the morning
to pre-occupy the day with study and prayer, he
then passed out into his parish, so that men said
of him forty years later, " He seemed to be
always praying, always preaching, always visiting
the sick, always catechising, always writing and
studying." His preaching made him the leading
churchman in that Galloway district, and his
studies resulted in 1636 in an elaborate book
against the advances of Arminianism, his *Exerci-
tationes Apologeticæ*, published at Amsterdam.
But the Scottish Church was by this time in
troubles other than theological, and Rutherfurd
had always been earnest in her cause. James had
restored the bishops, and the Bishop of Galloway
under Charles I. now insisted that the minister of
Anwoth should conform to the ceremonies. He
refused, and after a three days' trial in Edinburgh
before a court whose jurisdiction he questioned, he
was banished to Aberdeen, and prohibited from
exercising his ministerial office under pain of
rebellion. From September 1636 to February

1638 he remained in the north, flooding Scotland with letters, planning books of theology, disputing with Episcopalian doctors and conscientious Brownists, and drawn more and more into the national conflict which culminated in the Glasgow Assembly of 1638. That Assembly, which swept away the Bishops, of course restored Rutherfurd to Anwoth, but its successor in 1639 appointed him Professor of Divinity at St. Andrews, notwithstanding that he was at the same time called by the Magistrates of Edinburgh to be one of the ministers of this city. In 1639, too, the northern forces crossed the border, with their "brave new colour, stamped with the Scottish arms, and the motto, *For Christ's Crown and Covenant*, in golden letters." The covenant, so championed, was by this time safe against the tyranny of the king. But a new danger to it, or at least to its narrower interpretation, appeared in the views of the Independents, and Rutherfurd, who at first opposed vexing their representatives here by civil or ecclesiastical legislation, directed against them in 1642 his *Peaceable and Temperate Plea for Paul's Presbyterie in Scotland*.[1] That same year the

---

[1] The title commences in a "modest and brotherly" way, but it of course adds, "Wherein our Discipline is demonstrated to be the true apostolic way of Divine Truth."

Westminster Assembly was called by the two
Houses to meet in London, and in 1643 Rutherfurd went up as one of the eight Scottish Commissioners. He remained till 1647, not only
taking a zealous and important share in the work
of the Assembly, and preaching in the Scots
London Congregation, and occasionally before the
Parliament, but active also with his pen. In 1644
he published *The Due Right of Presbyteries*, a
second learned quarto in favour of our "classic
hierarchy" or hierarchy of "classes" or courts.
In the same fruitful year he gave to the world *Lex
Rex*. In 1645 he issued his *Trial and Triumph
of Faith;* a volume of sermons preached first in
Anwoth and then in London, on the Syrophenician
woman and her story. In 1646 appeared another
quarto on the *Divine Right of Church Government
and Excommunication*, with a brief tractate added,
" Of Scandall and Christian Libertie ; " and in
1647, *Christ Dying and Drawing Sinners to
Himself*, being, like the book of 1645, a volume
of practical sermons, of course with "some necessary digressions for the times." But he now

Two of the chapters contain suggestive matter as to separation in a church and from a church, and the whole subject
of scandal and separation is frequently handled in our
author's writings.

returned to Scotland and to St. Andrews, where, in addition to the ordinary work of a professor of divinity and minister of the city, he became Principal of the New College and Rector of the University. And all this was not enough for him. In 1648 he published a large and learned book against Antinomianism, entitled, *A Survey of the Spiritual Antichrist.* It was followed in 1649 by *A Free Disputation against Pretended Liberty of Conscience* and the various abettors of that rising heresy. One of the most respectable of these, Oliver Cromwell, found himself at this time called in the course of Providence, and under the orders of the Honourable House, to interfere in the affairs of Scotland, and did so with great energy on the fields of Preston and Dunbar. A few months after this last event, about Christmas of 1649, Charles Stuart, afterwards Charles II., appeared at St. Andrews, on his way to be crowned and to swear the covenant at Scone, and we are told that " Mr. Samuell Rutherfurde had a speche to him in Latin, running mutch upon what was the dewty of kings." One duty of kings is to unite their subjects, and Charles at this time took into his service not a few of the cavaliers who in Scotland had previously opposed the Covenant —an act which at once split the Church into

Resolutioners and Protesters, Rutherfurd being
the most irreconcilable of Protesters against that
amalgamation, and against General Assemblies
which countenanced it. Cromwell disposed of our
covenanted king and of his amalgamated sup-
porters somewhat prematurely at Worcester in
September 1651, but the feud in the Church lasted
to the end of Rutherfurd's life, and long after. In
that Worcester year Rutherfurd boiled down part
of his divinity lectures into a very tough "Dis-
putatio Scholastica" on Divine Providence, with
certain Metaphysical Disquisitions appended,[1] and
also declined an invitation to a second Dutch
theological chair—this time at Utrecht. In 1655
he wrote a book called *The Covenant of Life
Opened*, of much interest theologically; and in
1658 there followed *A Survey of the Survey of
that Sum of Church Discipline*, penned by some
Connecticut Independent in the rising New

---

[1] These Disquisitions fully deserve their epithet, being
" De Ente," " De Possibili," " De Dominio Dei in Entia *et
non entia*," etc. In the dedication to his students, he says
that it was now nearly fifteen years since he had sung a
farewell song to Academic strife, and his hesitation in
again pushing out his frail skiff (with no literary sail to
help it) into that forgotten sea, is founded on his having
"grown old, or at least grown rusty, in the absence of
controversy," *in desuetudine disputandi!*

England commonwealth.[1] At least one more
book of controversy, an *Examination of Arminianism*, in 700 pages, was built up in that St.
Andrews study, but it was not given to the world
till several years after Rutherfurd's approaching
death; and the last volume which was published
by himself came out in 1659 under the more
attractive title of *Influences of the Life of Grace.*
In 1660 King Charles was restored, and in 1661
the author of *Lex Rex*, cited to appear at Edinburgh on a charge of high treason, made answer
from his deathbed, "I behove to obey my *first*
summons." That summons to a higher bar laid
almost the first arrest on the swift keen hurrying
life. It gave Rutherfurd leisure to die, and while
the sky of Scotland was darkening all around, on
that chamber in St. Andrews there fell the light
that never was on land or sea.

A crowded life ! A life filled with all the intenser
interests of its time, and straining to meet them
with the whole armour of culture which the time
could give. Now, how came that hard and

[1] Mr. Thomas Hooker, of whose learning and piety
Rutherfurd speaks in a way honourable to both. The
preface also contains the usual protest against the spirit
of controversy, "as if that were the choicest verity which
the man's own engine " (*ingenium*) "hath taken out of an
adversary's hand with his sword and with his bow."

strenuous soil to burst into the pale gold blossoms
and consummate flower of love ?

There will always be men to find in the facts of
Rutherfurd's life a certain strangeness and incon-
gruity. Had these facts been otherwise,—had the
author of those Letters been a recluse, an enthu-
siast, or a dreamer ; a man living in advance of his
time, or living in a time gone by ; a dweller in soft
raiment and in king's houses on the one hand, or
clothed in camel's hair and making his lodge in the
wilderness on the other,—had any of these been
the case, we should not have felt it strange. Had
it been even some rude child of nature and of the
soil, a ploughman by his Scottish furrow or milk-
maid in her Highland strath—him or her we
might permit to rise at any moment far above us
on the wings of devotion and genius, much like
that plain brown bird which makes its bed in the
heather at our feet, but soars straight up and up
till the very heart of heaven palpitates with its
song. All that we could readily conceive. But a
politician and an ecclesiastic, a dialectician and a
polemic—how came *he* to be in our literature like
an unbodied joy whose race after two centuries is
but began ? The question will require a further
and discriminating consideration. But it may be
said at once and on the threshold, that they have

strangely forgotten history who question whether
an ecclesiastic and theologian, even of the most
dialectical order, can be at the same time a singer
or a saint. Let us recall only how among the
foremost hymn-writers of the middle age stand the
great scholastic Aquinas, and the great churchman
Bernard. And if there are those who decline to
receive even facts of history without some
suggested reason, let them be content with a story
which has floated down from the same shadowy
time :—

It was evening in the convent, and one brother
still knelt in his cell. Day after day, with fasting
and prayer, he had waited—hour after hour of this
day he has waited and watched, to see, in some
transcendent manifestation, a vision of Christ.
And now, at last, a light, a form, a face ! It is the
Lord Himself ! But at that moment comes sharp
and clear the convent bell,—the bell that calls the
poor and hungry to be fed at the convent door,
and calls him, the servitor appointed for that
task, to dispense the dole. Shall he go, or stay ?
Slowly, sadly, but with unreverted face, he leaves
his room ; and not till his whole work is done, not
till the last feeble and querulous and thankless
applicant has been served as often as he seems to
need, not till then does he set his feet to return.

But at last with slow feet and sinking heart he
does return to his desolate room, and as those feet
touch the threshold, lo ! again the gleam, the glory,
the Vision ! And as he prostrates himself, this
voice comes to him, " Because thou wentest, I
stayed. Hadst thou stayed, I should have
departed ! "

But we must look more narrowly into our
problem. For, whatever may have been true of
other men, there is a certain paradox in the case of
Rutherfurd. It is with him no mere collision
between opposing duties. There was indeed no
opposition in his case between the work to which
he was called externally, and his own inward
impulses and desires. The contrast which at once
strikes every one in the life of Rutherfurd was the
index of a deeper contrast in his character. But
that inward schism was strong and startling. It
looks sometimes as if there were two men in him.
One was the man whom all know in his letters,—
ardent, aspiring, and unworldly, impatient of earth,
intolerant of sin, rapt into the continual con-
templation of one unseen Face, finding his history
in its changing aspect and his happiness in its
returning smile. The other man was the intellectual gladiator, the rejoicing and remorseless
logician, the divider of words, the distinguisher

of thoughts, the hater of doubt and ambiguity, the scorner of compromise and concession, the incessant and determined disputant, the passionate admirer of sequence and system and order, in small things as in great,—in the corner of the corner of an argument, as in the mighty world outside with its orbits of the Church and of the State.

Now this twofold activity separates Rutherfurd from a particular type of excellence, by no means uncommon in our age. We may all have known men in whom a tender, aspiring, and somewhat feminine nature was combined with a certain limitation on the intellectual side. The limitation may have been original and connate. Or it may, on the other hand, have been superinduced and cherished (as, for example, by a passion for orthodoxy in matters of science or orthodoxy in matters of religion), with a corresponding growth of fixed and hard lines in the mind. Yet hard and strict as we may choose to think the mental environment of such men, the moral altitude to which they rise is often simply admirable. It seems sometimes almost as if they were constructed on the principle of the fountain, —the narrower the orifice, the higher the jet. I have said there is something feminine in such characters, and they certainly have in many cases a great attraction for the feminine nature and a great sympathy with it. Rutherfurd had both of these. Among the devout and honourable women of Scotland were his most intimate and most faithful friends; and when he sits down, as he sometimes does, to pour out his heart to a new correspondent whom he has never personally met, because they are both, as he puts it, "father's children," you are not surprised to discover that the new-found child is generally of the more appreciative sex, a sister of the one family rather than a brother. Of course in all such cases, and in this case eminently, the great attraction is the positive one, the moral height and purity of the man. But where such purity of heart is combined with fixed ideas and fast lines in the mind, the combination has an apparent strength which attracts and impresses the timid onlookers. Ordinarily, however, it does so by appealing to the reposeful and conservative instinct. But in Rutherfurd the case is not quite so. There is nothing reposeful about his intellect, and no atmosphere of conservatism about the man. His logic is active, his orthodoxy is aggressive, and his life is a kind of double whirlwind, the currents of its lower or intellectual region circling incessantly

according to their own laws, with a certain
independence of all that agitates with storm or
splendour the spiritual heights above. Now this
fact, that Rutherfurd's logic is masculine and
aggressive rather than feminine and conservative,
seems to me not only interesting but important.
For if it deprives us of the power of comparing
him with individual men around, it at once forces
upon us a parallel with our country as a whole.

Scotland differs from many other countries, and
in particular from England, in being more restless,
more argumentative, and more controversial.
And this is not simply because we are more self-
willed, more determined to carry our point and
have our own way. That also may be true. But
there is a mental as well as moral reason for it.
Scotsmen delight far more in the exercise of thinking for its own sake, and they do so when the
thinking takes the form of abstract speculation as
well as of practical discussion. It follows that, as
a nation, we have a passion for the form as well
as the matter of truth—sometimes, perhaps,
rather for the form than the matter. It follows,
too, that there is a difference in the method and
order of our mental procedure. In Scotland the
mind acts upon its subject : in England the subject
acts upon the mind. And the result is not always

in our favour. In Scotland there is at all times more thinking; but perhaps in England there is, upon the whole, more thought. At all events the slow, helpless, instinctive way in which the English mind lies open to a subject or an idea, and lets it grow gradually into its just proportions, produces in the long-run some riper and richer intellectual results than any which our more active manipulation has as yet to show. Now, these national characteristics existed in Scotland two centuries ago as they do now, and Rutherfurd was an eminent illustration of them. He was a born logician, and dealt far less with matter than with form. In his study he lived in a world of words; and the words to him represented ideas which constrained his conscience and his heart. Meantime the world of facts outside was changing very rapidly, and the changing facts did not fit into his unchanging form. But so much the worse for them, and for those whom they led astray.

And this leads us to Rutherfurd as a controversialist. As such he had some great excellencies. His acuteness, candour, courage, industry, learning, conscientiousness, and magnanimity, no less than his love of country and fear of God, come out in every one of his volumes. But he had some great shortcomings, closely connected with that of which

I have already spoken. I do not conceive myself qualified to deal with his properly theological discussions. But his continual attacks upon some probably very good men of the time, who were held to be "theoretical Antinomians," on the one hand, and on some, on the other, such as in my boyhood I have heard discriminatingly defended as "serious Arminians," all show one defect. It was a shortcoming of the age, and one in which our century has an enormous advantage. Rutherfurd, in dealing with opponents, never *put himself in their place.* He scarcely ever tried to do it, and does not seem to have acknowledged it as a duty of controversy. But it is a duty, and it is at least an enormous advantage, in dealing with opponents, to seek to occupy their point of view; in particular, to occupy that point of view in which their conclusions commence to branch off from what we hold in common. To put one's self in an opponent's place is the way, first, to get all the good from him that we can, and, secondly, to do all the good to him that we can. It is of course not the logical way of dealing with him. But it is quite consistent with good logic; and it keeps before us certain considerations which mere logic is sure to omit. For example, all the necessary consequences of an opinion are deducible from it

by logic. But all those consequences are not to
be charged upon the man who holds the opinion,
as if he held them also. Rutherfurd continually
omits to notice this, and on one occasion when it
is suggested that it is not charitable to impute
to certain English writers the extravagances of
American familists, he roundly answers that,
seeing these Englishmen openly held the same
theoretically Antinomian doctrines, " they are to
be charged with all those, till they clear themselves or refute those blasphemies." Another
illustration of the same tendency is his treatment
of the question of the fundamentals of religion.
He is full of suggestive distinctions upon this ; but
he has no hesitation in including among matters
of faith, " 1. Fundamental points ; 2. Superstruc-
tions builded upon fundamentals ; 3. *Circa funda-
mentalia*, things about matters of Faith." Are
wrong opinions as to these last sins ? His answer
is, that " God hath in His word determined all
controversies not fundamental, as well as fundamental ; " and the not believing of what God hath
revealed must be a sin and transgression of a
divine law.[1] The extreme awkwardness of this
only comes out when we remember Rutherfurd's
views as to toleration and the Civil Magistrate.

[1] *Due Right of Presbyteries*, p. 361.

" There be divers opinions," he says, " which are
not against points fundamental, which being professed are sins against our brother and the
churches. *Ergo*, many opinions not against points
fundamental, if professed, are censurable by the
Church, and *punishable by the Magistrate.*"[1] He
instances the destruction of Sodom as a revealed
truth, the denial of which in a Christian country
would give the criminal prosecutor a right to
interfere. Now all this has a bearing, to which
we shall afterwards refer, on the critical events of
Rutherfurd's time, and the want of success of our
country in dealing with that time. But at
present I adduce them as singular illustrations of
that blind passion for logic which led him to
ignore the different values of facts outside, and
invariably to deal with opponents from his point
of view rather than from theirs.

One remark, however, I must make, and it goes
deeper than mere illustrations. It is a little hard
to ask a man to put himself in the place of his
opponents, who has no power of putting himself in
the place even of his friends. And I am afraid
this must be said of Rutherfurd. He is anything
but a hard or unfeeling man: he is even a
thoroughly unselfish man ; but he is an unselfish

[1] *Due Right of Presbyteries*, p. 363.

egoist. That is to say, he does not put himself in the place of others. Even his sympathy with them is merely a pouring forth of his own feelings in accordance with what he assumes must be their state of mind. He does not inquire what that state of mind is, nor does he, as some men do, feel it by a certain instinct. He does not understand the people themselves. He does not even try to understand them. He does not make you understand them. Rutherfurd's Letters, had they come from the hands of some men, would have been a wonderful amphitheatre of the Scotsmen and Scotswomen around him in that very living time. As it is, it is a gallery of dummies. We do not know one of them, and it is doubtful whether he knew one of them. Take a closer circle still. He was twice married ; his mother lived with him for six years after his first wife's death ; and his second wife is said by a competent witness to have been " a woman of such worth, that I never knew any among men exceed him, nor any among women exceed her." Yet of these three women that indefatigable pen reveals absolutely nothing. He had nine children, and his letters extend from three years after the birth of the eldest, to six years after the birth of the youngest. But we know more of the birds who built in the kirk of

Anwoth, than of the bairns who played in the manse. Now all this reveals a real defect and a serious incapacity. In his family and in his parish, at least, it is plain that Rutherfurd did not give himself to understand those around him. He was, no doubt, in his private life careful and exemplary. He was more—he was impressive. But that means that he impressed others. It does not mean that others impressed him. It is plain indeed that they did not, and that he did not greatly desire that they should, or feel any necessity that they should. He never *waited* for others to influence or to impress him. I am not prepared to say that he had not the humility necessary for that. But he had not the intellectual and moral patience for it, though he had the moral unselfishness. And so he poured himself forth on all around indiscriminately, giving but not receiving, teaching but not taught.

Now if that is a real defect even in a man's private life, it is a most serious disability when he comes to deal with public affairs. I do not believe in the right of any man to pronounce judgment on his time, or the movements of his time (and Rutherfurd is often very strong and peremptory in such judgments), except upon condition of his first understanding his time. And I do not see

how any man is to understand his time, to know
what it has and what it lacks, what the State
craves at his hands, and "what Israel ought to
do," unless he first studies to understand his time
—studies it, that is, with sympathy, with tolerance, and with insight—at least, with that re-
spectful consideration for the views and wishes of
men around·him, with which he feels it right and
natural that men around him should study him.
We shall, I think, find that the want of this, to
a large extent, explains the very partial success
which a man with the high qualities of Rutherfurd had in public affairs. But what I wish to
remark at present is, that it goes far to explain
the abiding inward schism—the permanent split
and severance in the man himself—which struck
us at the first. Many young men commence with
such a disjunction in their life ; with a keen
interest in ideals and abstractions, but wholly
unconnected with reality as it exists around them.
But they are not left to that unreal state of
things. Dealing with others, meeting with others,
mixing with others, in family life, in friendly life,
in public life, is God's ordinance for this. It is
the bridge by which the gap was intended to be
spanned. But no bridge is of use unless you cross
it. Even a divine ordinance is worthless, so long

as men do not bend heart and mind to its obedience.   And as Rutherfurd intellectually dealt
with form rather than with matter, so in practical
life he persistently dealt with ideas rather than
with men.

There is one indication of this too significant
not to be noticed.   I allude to the style of metaphor which at the present day interferes with
the usefulness of all his popular writings.   It is
very strange that Rutherfurd, who early in his
life had received a sharp lesson as to carelessness
in this region, should be so uniformly and frankly
incautious.   No doubt others in his age (and it
was a grave and manly age) used the like phrases.
And in other times men like the great St.
Bernard, in his sermons on The Song, have employed a similar vehicle for their thoughts, and
used it with much greater elaboration.   But
Bernard, statesman and world-mover as he was,
was after all a man of the cloister, and had the
disabilities of his profession.   Rutherfurd, as a
man immersed in ordinary life, should have had
quicker instincts of common sense.   But the truth
is, Rutherfurd was not immersed in ordinary life.
He was in the world but not of it in more senses
than one.   To say the whole thing in a word, no
one can give Samuel Rutherfurd his place in a

Succession stretching over all the centuries without recognising that he was in nature and temper a monk. He was a monk in a Scottish parish, and in a Scottish manse. He had all the unworldly purity and aspiration of the cloister; but he had also somewhat of its incapacity to discern that which is safe and seemly for those without the walls.

And surely this special point is but a small fragment of the great parallel which we are bound to recognise in this case with the cloister. We have nothing in Scotland equal to the conjunction found in Rutherfurd of intense scholasticism with intense devotion. It was St. Thomas and St. Francis under one hood. But still it was a conjunction, not a union. And during the long ages of the Latin Church precisely the same conjunction was found in many a solitary, who for lack of the fusing influences of life was never able to unite the two sides of his being. And so it was with Rutherfurd. We began with saying that there were two men in him. I have now to say that the two men—the two halves of the man— were never made into one effective whole. To the very last the scholasticism and the devotion, however closely intermixed, are never fused together; in Bacon's phrase, they are iron and clay—"they cleave, but they do not incorporate."

All this, I think, was necessary to be said. But history, and the evangelical succession which flows through history, are more interested in the other side, and, of course, in the first place, in the *Letters*. A book which even in our own century has been edited by men so representative as Thomas Erskine of Linlathen and Dr. Andrew Bonar does not need analysis or reproduction. But it is singular to what an extent its power has been acknowledged by men not all of the same school. The "Remains" or table-talk of Richard Cecil, the English divine of a previous generation, are a little forgotten now, but in masculine strength and hard-headedness they are rather above than below the taste of the present age. Yet as to Rutherfurd's Letters he breaks out in one place, " It is one of my classics. Were truth the beam, I have no doubt that if Homer, and Virgil, and Horace, and all that the world has agreed to idolise, were weighed against that book, they would be lighter than vanity. He is a real original." Take a greater man still, Richard Baxter, Rutherfurd's contemporary and opponent. He once said to Principal Carstairs, " Hold off the Bible, such a book as Mr. Rutherfurd's Letters

the world never saw the like."[1] All I shall say
of them at this point is, that they represent his
whole life. There is a great gush from Aberdeen
in the year 1637 ; but sixty-five previous, and
eighty which follow that date, cover the thirty-
four years between his ordination and death.
And they are all like each other, and all like him.

Our next step, therefore, is from his letters to his
sermons. Rutherfurd was one of the most famous
men of the pulpit in his day : "one of the most
moving and affectionate preachers in his time, or
perhaps in any age of the Church." And his
sermons were as incessant as his letters. When
a professor no less than when a pastor, in London
and St. Andrews as well as in his own parish by
the Solway, throughout his life indeed, with the
one exception of the time when he was a banished
minister in Aberdeen, he was "always preaching."
Take of the two sermon volumes he published that
which is less known, the book on *Christ Dying
and Drawing Sinners to Himself.* On almost the
first page which I open I find this sentence :—

"Would sinners but draw near, and come and
see this king Solomon in his chariot of love, and
behold his beauty, the uncreated white and red in

[1] "Which," our honest Principal added, "was a great
token and evidence to me of Mr. Baxter's true piety."

his countenance, he would draw souls to him.
There is omnipotency of love in his countenance ;
all that is said of him here are but created shadows :
ah ! words are short to express his nature, person,
office, loveliness, desirableness.   What a broad and
beautiful face must he have, who with one smile
and one turning of his countenance looks upon all
in heaven and all in the earth, and casts a heaven
of burning love, east and west, south and north,
through heaven and earth, and fills them all ! "

That is the exact note which we all remember
as most frequent in the Letters, but indeed everything that is characteristic of them is to be found
in some part of this one volume of London Sermons.   I cannot forbear instancing another passage, prose monody, which recalls the music of a
well-known poem by the present laureate :—

" If it be so, that death, finding so precious a
surety, as Christ's princely and sinless soul, did
make Him obey the law of the land, ere He escaped
out of that land : what wonder that we die, who
are born in the land of death ?   All things under
the moon must be sick of vanity and death, when
the heir of all things, coming in amongst dying
creatures, out of dispensation, by law must die.
If the Lord's soul, and the soul of such a Lord die
and suffer wrath, then let the fair face of the

world, the heavens, look like the face of an old
man full of trembling, white hairs, and wrinkles—
then let man make for his long home, let time
itself wax old and grey-haired. Why should I
desire to stay here, when Christ could not but pass
away!—And if this spotless soul that never sinned
was troubled, what wonder then many troubles be
to the sinner? Our Saviour, who promiseth soul-
rest to others, cannot have soul-rest Himself ; His
soul is now on a wheel sore tossed. And all the
creatures are upon a wheel, and in motion; there
is not a creature since Adam sinned, sleepeth
sound. Weariness and motion is laid on moon
and sun, and all creatures on this side of the
moon.[1] Seas ebb and flow, and that's trouble ;
winds blow, rivers move, heavens and stars these
five thousand years, except one time, have not had
six minutes' rest ; living creatures walk apace
toward death ; kingdoms, cities, are on the wheel
of changes, up and down ; mankind run, and the
disease of body-trouble and soul-trouble is on them,

[1] Tennyson, on the other hand, complains that

> " While all things else have rest from weariness,
> We only toil."

But this is in the person of a lotus-eater, whose sympathy
with the bondage of the creation was perhaps less pene-
trating than that of Rutherfurd or Paul.

they are motion-sick, going on their feet, and kings cannot have beds to rest in. The great All of heaven and earth, since God laid the first stone of this wide hall, hath been groaning and weeping for the liberty of the sons of God. The figure of the passing-away world is like an old man's face, full of wrinkles, and foul with weeping: we are waiting till Jesus shall be revealed from heaven, and shall come and wipe the old man's face. Every creature here is on its feet, none of them can sit or lie. But Christ's soul now is above trouble, and rests sweetly in the bosom of God. Trouble souls, rejoice in hope." [1]

Forty years before Samuel Rutherfurd preached these words in St. Andrew's Kirk in London, he fell into a well when playing with other children in their native parish of Nisbet. They ran away for assistance, and on their return they found the boy sitting on a green knoll, unhurt but dripping, and to their question how he had got out he answered, " A bonnie white man came and drew him out of the well!" It was no doubt some fair-haired shepherd of Teviotdale who passed that way; but those who heard and read his preaching in after days loved to think that the bonnie white man was a stranger from the fair country, in that

[1] *Christ Dying*, p. 13.

garb which is "candor here and lustre there,"[1]
sent not only to draw the young Rutherfurd out
of the pit, but to put a new song in his mouth,
or at least to touch the child's lips with the wild
honey of the unknown land which was yet afar
off. For through thirty years of preaching in
later days, a fragrance of heaven clung to his lips.
All the accounts agree in this, and agree, too, as
to the centre of that constant attraction. "I
went to St. Andrews," said an English merchant
in the Protectorate, "and there heard a little fair
man ; and he showed me the loveliness of Christ."
An old Morayshire minister who survived the
Revolution, looking back over his lifetime, said,
"I have known many great and good ministers in
this church, but for such a piece of clay as Mr.
Rutherfurd was, I never knew one in Scotland
like him, to whom so many great gifts were
given." How did that piece of clay strike
contemporaries ? Other observers give us (in
Wodrow's *Analecta*) what amounts to a description
of him. It is a pen-sketch which is invaluable,
for no portrait of Rutherfurd has come down to
us. "He had two quick eyes,[2] and when he

---

[1] Herrick's *White Island.*

[2] So the legends of other child-poets—especially of
Horace, also an *animosus infans*—"two quick eyes."

walked it was observed that he held aye his face
upward and heavenward." " He had a strange
utterance in the pulpit, a kind of *skreigh* that I
never heard the like." " Many a time I thought
he would have flown out of the pulpit when he
came to speak of Jesus Christ." We can still see
him—the little fair man, with the falsetto in his
voice, and the quick heavenward eyes—heavenward, even when he is pelting Mr. Baxter or
pounding Dr. Crisp; but when he leaves them and
all things else to speak of his Master within that
shining veil, it seems now as if he would himself
follow those upward eyes—the whole man is on
tiptoe for the sky![1]

Here, then, we have the Rutherfurd of the
letters almost bodily in his sermons. But that
is not the only thing that is there. The other
Rutherfurd is in the sermons too. When he
stepped into his pulpit in Anwoth or St. Andrews,
his congregation knew they were to get from him
all that was in him. And his sermons contain—
almost every one of his lectures at least contains
—not Rutherfurd the poet and evangelist alone,
but Rutherfurd the theologian and systematic, the

[1] " St. Francis gesticulated with his hands and feet, as
though on the point of taking flight."—RENAN'S *New
Studies*, p. 321.

casuist and *ductor dubitantium*, the debater and controversialist, the churchman and preacher to the times. And all this a congregation in those days expected and demanded. These were all subjects in which they took a deep interest, and they insisted upon their being discussed, and discussed in the pulpit. Whatever may be the improved rule of the days to come, it was never the custom of Scotland in the time gone by (as it has become to a large extent in England, and still more in Germany) to feed grown men on Sundays with spoon-meat or with slops. " They gave the people of their best ; " they fed them with meat as well as milk, not on Thursday, Friday, and Saturday alone, in books and magazines, in news-rooms and in lecture-rooms, but on the day which God had made, and in that house of God which, whatever else it is, was built to be the pillar and ground of the truth. I do not say that they always did this wisely. I do not say at present that they did it successfully. I do not even say that they did it upon a right method ; that the outward and inward, the life of religion and the science of religion, were always joined together in those days on any true internal principle of connection. But they were joined. They were connected. They were continually connected, in every book and in every sermon. Heart and head were united even in the popular and pulpit theology of our fathers, more heart and more head too than we in modern days count ourselves worthy to receive. The theological and controversial digressions which fill half the sermons of the age, may not have been necessary in that form. But in some form they were necessary, for they represented the working of the pure minds of that time upon the subjects which most attract the human soul at all times. To the uneducated man in modern days, Arminianism and Antinomianism are mere big words which he finds himself rather tempted to look down upon. But to the student of history, they stand for permanent tendencies in the nature of man; tendencies which it is no more possible for the human being to escape than it is for the inhabitant of the tropics to escape from the regions south and north of the equator. Whether the theological equator runs exactly where our seventeenth century put it, or whether it was such a fixed line at all as was then supposed, may be questioned. But the intellectual excursions, the controversial raids which were made on both sides, largely fulfilled the purpose in that day of a mental discipline. They carried out into detail that masculine con-

ception of religion which was never wanting even
to the most emotional of the Puritans, but which
Rutherfurd especially might have been tempted
to forget. He never forgot it; and nothing is
clearer than that his remembrance was due, not
to his own intellectual tendencies alone, but to his
sense also of the permanent spiritual needs of
himself and his people. I have said earlier in
this paper that he had no great power of putting
himself in the mental position of others. It is the
more necessary to observe that that did not prevent him from feeling their great common needs
and sympathising with their great common
sorrows. "When one arm is broken off and
bleeds, it makes the other bleed with it," were the
words with which he called for a pen to write to
David Dickson on the death of a child. He had
the pastor's eye for those that were in trouble,
and the priest's heart for all that were out of the
way. "He was extremely and almost excessively
charitable" to the poor, and he used to say that
it had never been better with him than when in
Anwoth he sat on the mortar-stone at his own
door speaking about their souls to the beggars who
gathered around. Rutherfurd, as a pastor, lived
for others, not for himself, and (to return to the
point in hand) the long discussions which he

introduced into his sermons were not only intended
to meet the needs of his people, but were largely
successful in meeting them. The form of those
discussions may have been too scholastic and systematic, but scattered through them all there is
very much not only of stimulus for the mind, but
of nourishment for the heart and guidance for
the life.

From all this I think it follows that the contrast which now strikes us as existing between
Rutherfurd in his letters and Rutherfurd in his
books was not nearly so visible to men of his own
time. It was bridged over by the Rutherfurd of
the sermons. But it is high time to say also
that the conjunction of the two things—of the two
sides—in this one life is largely accounted for by
the necessities of the times. Rutherfurd, as we
saw, lived a quiet life in his own parish until the
questions which afterwards rent the State in
pieces invaded his retirement. The most peace-
loving parish minister may consent to take an
interest in public affairs when these threaten to
banish him (as they did some ministers whom we
remember) from his manse and his work. But
Rutherfurd did not need such a personal stimulus.
He was at no time a man of " a private spirit;"
and henceforth there was no repose for him,

because there was none for his Church. Charles
and Laud, the royal supremacy and a more than
English liturgy, came all down upon us together.
What was Scotland to do? Some Scotsmen knew
what to do. There were fools and fribbles in
plenty, but there were also men who could do and
dare and suffer, and take burden for others. But
the burden grew heavier and more complicated.
It was a simple thing for the Church to become
free, and to refuse to be governed by civil proclamation or by statute. But what if it wished
to be free, and at the same time to coerce others
by civil statute and proclamation? How were
those whom the bishops had oppressed as sectaries
in Galloway to subjugate the sectaries of Aberdeen? The Scottish Covenant was a noble
confession, but the imposition of it on all holders
of office was very like a forcing of conscience.
And all this difficulty became aggravated fourfold
when England came in. Even to have a common
sovereign was no easy problem for two nations,
one of whom held it its duty to defend, and the
other to decapitate him. But the church problem
was more complicated still. Both peoples belonged
to the Catholic Visible Church, in which Rutherfurd earnestly believed, and they were bound to
profess the Reformed faith together. The church

in both lands ought to stand on one platform :
and they set about constructing it. But some
men refused to stand on that platform, and insisted on their Christian right to stand separately.
Was this to be tolerated ? Of course it broke up
the whole fair fabric of uniformity. And that
fabric to Rutherfurd seemed very fair. He went
to England with a glowing sense of the unity of
the Christian Church on the one hand, and with
all his Scottish ideas of national oneness on the
other ; and now he who would have been content
to be "a common rough barrow-man in Anwoth,"
seemed called upon to build the very temple of
the Lord. His imagination caught flame : year
after year he gave himself and every faculty to
that magnificent undertaking ; and in volume
after volume we may trace the eager anticipation
that breaks forth in the motto to his *Due Right
of Presbyteries :* "Who is she that looketh forth
as the morning, fair as the moon, clear as the sun,
and terrible as an army with banners ? "

And he failed. For once in our history, Scotland had an opportunity of establishing its own
polity and its own ideas on the other side of the
border, and it failed. We did our best ; or, at
least, we did our utmost : and did not succeed.
In vain did Rutherfurd point out that "in God's

matters there be not, as in grammar, the positive
and comparative degrees : there are not here,
truth, and more true, and most true. Truth is in
an indivisible line, which hath no latitude, and
cannot admit of splitting." [1] Englishmen listened,
and did not exactly contradict. But they found
that truth, as it was seized hold of by their own
minds, *was* a good deal split up, and many of them
were disposed to keep fast hold each of that particular strand which God had put into his grasp,
and to let their neighbours do the like. Much
was accomplished in the way of union, no doubt.
We got a Confession and a Catechism. But the
authoritative erection of the presbyterian polity,
with Assemblies to govern it, was too much for
England, joined to us though it was, not only in a
" civil league," but also in a " religious covenant."
And soon that noble League and Covenant, binding together the stronger and weaker nations,
became a danger for Presbyterianism in Scotland.
" What a fearful judgment of God is this upon
us," says honest Baillie, " that, we thought, should
have bound the nations unseparably, is like to be
the first separation of them." We crowned our
young king at Scone, with the Covenant in one
hand, and in the other his claim to the crown

[1] Dedication of *Due Right of Presbyteries.*

which his father had just laid down with his life at Whitehall. England and its Lord General were forced in self-defence to attack us, and field after field "with blood of Scots embrued" were but the beginning of our discomfiture. Cromwell, indeed, having given us hard blows, followed them up with soft and rather incoherent words. We were not incoherent, even in defeat. We demonstrated in the clearest and most logical way that we were right, and that our platform was the only true, orderly, sensible, and scriptural way of managing a church and a nation. The Lord General did not always answer, and when he did he was often barely grammatical : only sometimes there was a pathetic outburst that came near to the heart of the matter. "I beseech you, in the bowels of Christ, think it possible you may be mistaken !" We sincerely thought otherwise; and the Commonwealth, recognising the painful honesty which afflicted us, took the mildest measures that were possible. But they were effectual measures. It shut up our Assembly and Parliament. It suspended our national independence. Not only had we failed in what we attempted in England, we now lost also that which we had possessed in Scotland. And Rutherfurd accepted it as absolute failure. "The Lord," he

says in one of his latest letters, " hath removed
Scotland's crown, for we owned not His crown.
We fretted at His Catholic government of the
world, and fretted that He would not be ruled and
led by us in breaking our adversaries, and He
maketh us to suffer and pine away in our
iniquities, under the broken government of His
house." And yet that time was prosperity compared with what followed. Rutherfurd, like many
religious men who have no gift of understanding
their age, was apt to speak peremptorily and even
prophetically about it; and he made many bad
shots in consequence. [1] But it needed, as he himself said when he lay down to die, no gift of
prophecy to see that dark days were then coming.
They came, and they deepened into the " killing
time; " and it was all the result, direct or indirect,
of our failure in the days of the Commonwealth.
England then needed our considerate sympathy,

---

[1] In the dedication to his sermons published in 1645, he
describes the temper of the age he lived in as " the declining temper of the world's worst time." It was the time
when his own principles were more successful than they
have been before or since ; the era which those who seek to
occupy his exact standpoint have always looked back to as
the one golden age of the Church of Scotland, and as the
only time when the world around it seemed prepared to
join that church's triumph.

if ever a nation did, and we did not give it. And
we needed the support and strength of England,
though we knew it not. So the time passed,
unredeemed, and when the Restoration came, it
was our act as truly as the act of our southern
neighbours, and the results fell most heavily on
us.

Now, one of the collateral questions suggested
by our subject is this. Assuming that all this
public action in Rutherfurd's time, and, in particular, on the part of Rutherfurd himself, resulted
in failure, was it a necessary failure? Was it a
mere misfortune and fatality? Or was it a grave
blunder and mistake, such as a later age—an age
which is yet to come—might avoid? Carlyle gives
a certain answer to this question, from the English
side, and from the point of view of a biographer.
"With Oliver Cromwell born a Scotsman, with a
Hero King and a unanimous Hero Nation at his
back, it might have been far otherwise" than it
was. "With Oliver born Scotch, one sees not but
the whole world might have become Puritan," and
Puritanism he has defined on the previous page,
somewhat too favourably, as "the attempt to
bring the divine law of the Bible into actual
practice in men's affairs on the earth." We may
admit that Cromwell made a mistake in not being

born a Scotsman, as we certainly made an immense mistake in not ardently adopting him into the family. But let us leave persons, and consider how we might have dealt with principles. I cannot help thinking that if Scotland and England in that age had simply broken the yoke of arbitrary power in Church and State, and got rid of the Royal supremacy in ecclesiastical matters, and of Prelacy as founded upon it, there was no insuperable obstacle thereafter. The difficulty was that we had to acknowledge the rights of minorities and of individuals, who were, as we thought, in the wrong, or who had not yet attained to be in the right. That difficulty, so far as regarded the great question between Independents and Presbyterians, might, I think, have been overcome, if not in the way in which it was actually smoothed over in England by Cromwell, by some similar plan of mutual forbearance. But it could not be done without abandoning that testimony against toleration in which, not Rutherfurd only, but the whole Scots Commissioners joined. It could scarcely be done without abandoning, even in Scotland, the right, dear to both sides, of forcing people in a parish to attend their parish church, and of treating Quakers and Separatists as enemies to the civil law. More than that. It

could not, I think, be done, or at least it could
not be carried out as a real and permanent experiment, without a change in the whole attitude
of mind of the men of that day—certainly in the
whole attitude of Rutherfurd's mind—to the doctrinal system, as well as the ecclesiastical. It was
not necessary that they should give up their own
belief either in the one system or the other, or
even that they should cease to hold them up as
the models to which men must ultimately come.
But what were they to do with those who in the
meantime did not attain to them ? Rutherfurd's
answer generally was, " You must believe in them,
for they are God's truth." But sometimes, when in
a conciliatory mood, his answer seems to be, " You
must believe in them, or reject them, and refute
them ; and here am I and a hundred others ready to
discuss them with you from morn till night." And
he was by no means prepared for the answer, which
was in the hearts of many and on the lips of some,
" No, we will do neither the one nor the other.
We shall not accept your system. And we shall
not reject it. We will not even consider it. We
have our own religious questions which interest us,
and we must attack them under God's leading and
in our own way." There were many " Seekers " in
London and in England in those days, besides the

sect known by that name, and our Scots Commissioners did not err much when they accused the
whole people whom they met of being tainted with
the same insubordinate spirit. Where they did
err was in not seeing, first, that such objectors
were standing on their right—their absolute and
God-given right ; and, secondly, that the preval-
ence of such a spirit, if it brought its own dangers
along with it, was also a sign of infinite hope.
Rutherfurd, of course, would not see the hope : he
saw only the dangers to his system. He and his
friends pressed their views upon the English
people with the same pertinacity and almost the
same authority with which they would have
ignored the rights of a younger generation of their
own countrymen (for every new generation comes
fresh into the world, and a Scotsman is born as
ignorant as John Milton). With all my belief in
Presbyterianism,—nay, because of my belief in
Presbyterianism as the inevitable future of the
self-governing English race and of the Church
universal,—I sympathise with the whole of the
indignant remonstrance :—

> " Dare you for this adjure the civil sword
>   To force our consciences which Christ set free,
>   And ride us with a classic hierarchy
>   Taught ye by mere A. S. and Rutherford ? "

And so Rutherfurd rhymes for ever to the "civil sword," and his failure in that crowning public aim is recorded in literature as in history. In other things—even in other public things, and in the great Scottish duty of his time—he did not fail. But even on our side of the border, as in the continued and repeated breach with the Resolutioners, the same temper reappears which we have seen in his dealings with England and the Independents,—followed here also by unfortunate results. And in both cases the failure is clearly connected with something which we have sought to trace in the man. We must ask therefore with regard to the man, as we have done with regard to the enterprise in which he was engaged, Was failure necessary? Once when he was preaching, and had suddenly left the dissensions of the time to speak of the scent of the fair "Rose of Sharon," the Laird of Glanderston was heard to say in a loud whisper, "Ay, now you are right—hold you there!" And undoubtedly that loud whisper has been the verdict of posterity. It is perhaps substantially true, but it must be taken with a certain modification of meaning. If any one thinks that Samuel Rutherfurd should have confined himself to that side of his nature, or that side of his preaching, the answer is that it was impossible—impossible and undesirable. His public duties and relations to others, his position as a minister and a Scotsman, nay, as an educated man and a thinker, made it impossible. He could not do it without ignoring the whole world of duty on the one hand, and the whole world of truth on the other. But if what is meant is, that this was the highest and the central thing in Rutherfurd, it is most true, and it instantly raises another question. It is the business of that which is highest to rule, not to reign merely but to govern —why did it not seem to do so here? All Rutherfurd's energy in other directions only amounts to talent, while in his letters he is a religious genius. But genius is a plastic and a vital power; its prerogative, and therefore I think its duty, is to unify that which is broken, and to quicken that which is dead. Was it not possible for Rutherfurd, first as a theologian and then as an ecclesiastic, to have worked out from his own centre— from that glowing apprehension of Christ and the presence of Christ which filled him? Was it not the business of that central fire to fuse the cold masses around it, that so they might all flow into their native mould and assume their appropriate form?

It might have been, perhaps: and to some

4

extent it ought to have been. But it was not
even attempted. That internal connection was
not the manner of the age. Had it been attempted we might have lost something, but also
gained. Rutherfurd's words might no doubt have
thus been pruned, and his soaring "thoughts
condensed within his soul and changed to purpose
strong." And that theological purpose would
have left him no time for one-half of his work
in controversial detail. But, on the other hand,
his life would not make some men in modern days
feel as if they were handed a harsh and astringent
cup, with a lump of sugar at the bottom. And
above all, it would not have presented that aspect
in his own time. That would have made room
for a diffused and pervasive charity to Royalists,
brotherhood with Independents, reconciliation with
Resolutioners. Had that astonishingly discursive
intellect been only concentrated, so as to unfold
that which was in Rutherfurd's own heart,—nay,
to unfold Him who was in it in the form in which
He was there,—I believe the result might have
been memorable;—though doubtless after all it
might have failed to reconcile that distracted time.

Ah! we find it so easy to be wiser than our
fathers were. You see we have this great advantage over them : we can vary and amend the

· questions which are to be answered, whereas they
had to answer them as they were put by Providence,
and as they were bequeathed to them by their
fathers. I have suggested that the question of
principle, even with regard to that crowning of the
edifice which our fathers looked for in England,
was not quite incapable of solution. But practically, as all those external questions came up to
be dealt with by them, it was about the most
hopeless business that ever heroic men broke their
hearts upon. You know Carlyle's way of putting
it : " Given a Divine law of the Bible on the one
hand, and a Stuart King, Charles First *or* Charles
Second, on the other ; alas, did history ever
present a more irreducible case of equations in
this world?" But the personal difficulty was the
smallest part of it. With any English monarch,
with any British legislature, the question would
have been equally hopeless to men encompassed
with the hard traditions of feudalism and ecclesiasticism by which our fathers were bound. And
no one, I think, who looks in detail into that history can doubt the unselfishness and magnanimity
with which, amid the cruel necessities of the time,
they gave themselves to their work, ever laying
the heavier burdens inward and outward upon
themselves, and seeking to be foremost only in

suffering for the public weal. But if we have any
difficulty about the estimate, there is an easy way
to test it. *We* have got out of all those strict
and strait necessities, we have no rigid barriers
imposed upon us from the present or the past, we
are enlightened and free—what use do we make
of our advantages? Yes, freedom is a great
virtue, but "you of the virtue, how strive you?"
Ah! it is not for us in our languorous time, when
every door opens at a touch, and every barrier
falls with a push—it is not for us, so backward to
act and so slow to suffer, to speak with easy lips
of the failure of those of old!

But did they fail after all? Rutherfurd
thought he did, and said so. But men are sometimes not the best judges of that which themselves
have done, not even at the close of life. God does
not always pay wages on the Saturday night;
and He never pays in the precise coin which we
have taught ourselves to expect. It is strange to
see how many of the men who have done the
greatest things in this world were brought to the
verge of some good land, and perhaps saw it with
their eyes, but were not allowed to go over.
Luther's life ended when his Germany was broken
and miserable, and we can understand how even
that strong soul was heard to say long before,

"The world seems to me like a decayed house,
David and the prophets being the spars, and
Christ the main pillar in the midst that supports
all." And again, " Ah ! how willingly would I
now die, for I am faint and overwrought, and at
this time I have a joyful and peaceable conscience." Scotland was never in a more torn and
distracted state than when John Knox lay down
to die, calling upon " his dear brethren " to pray
with him " that God in His mercy will please to
put an end to my long and painful battle, . . .
for as the world is weary of me, so am I of it."
So it was with the last days of Henderson, and
of Rutherfurd, as well as of thousands of our
unknown countrymen whose record is on high.
All these Scotsmen, though they obtained a good
report through faith, received. *not* the promise,
God having provided some better thing for us,
that they without us should not be made perfect !
But they planted the strong roots of our liberties,
and we at the best can but reap the harvest of
a field which other men have tilled and sown.
Those who come after us to the latest age will
gather the fruit, not of the prayers only, but of
the efforts, of men who two hundred years ago
passed away with unsatisfied eyes from their
broken work, the hot heart stilled after the storms

of life, and the seal of death upon the faithful
brow.

But Rutherfurd at least did not pass away with
unsatisfied eyes. The seal set upon his closing life
shines before us all, and no man can read failure
there. He does not fail who, when earthly things
are breaking and crumbling around him, finds
himself suddenly in the centre and heart of all,
and sees the Face which his whole life has sought
to see. For this after all was what that life had
sought. Not earthly peace, not success or honour,
not the prosperity even of his church, not wisdom
even divine, was what he had desired. He sought
above all things to see one Face which is yet
unseen. And because he desired this one thing,
and sought it, with no consciousness of desert,
yet in painful paths of uprightness, the vision was
not denied to him which other eyes have missed.
How often from many a dull house in Scotland
and many a decorous manse has gone up the cry,
" Lo, these many years do I serve thee, neither
transgressed I at any time thy commandment :
and yet—thou never gavest me a kid ! " But this
man, who thought much of Christ and little of
others and less of himself, and who often transgressed even that eleventh commandment of love [1]

[1] The tradition is well known, of Archbishop Usher

in passionate striving after an unwise ideal—this
man had the ring put upon his hand and shoes
upon his feet, and was feasted in Christ's palace of
Aberdeen ! So it had been even of old, and now
when he had nothing left to desire but that which
he had always desired, his Desire came to him
unsought. I do not quote those last words which
have passed in our time into Christian song.
And I abstain now, as before, from citing the
letters in which his latest aspirations are so often
anticipated. But I take instead a passage from
the volume of sermons which we did not formerly
quote, his *Trial and Triumph of Faith*, or rather
from its Dedication : —

"There is not a rose out of heaven, but there is
a blot and thorn growing out of it, except that
one only rose of Sharon, which blossometh out
glory. Every leaf of that rose is a heaven, and
serveth 'for the healing of the nations;' every
white and red in it is incomparable glory; every
act of breathing out its smell, from everlasting to
everlasting, is spotless and unmixed happiness.
Christ is the outset, the master-flower, the un-

appearing *incognito* at the " mortar-stone " of the Anwoth
Manse, and when the guest was asked by Rutherfurd at
the nightly catechising how many commandments there
were, he answered, " Eleven ! "

created garland of heaven, the love and joy of men
and angels. But the fountain-love, the fountain-
delight, the fountain-joy of men and angels is
more; for out of it floweth all the seas, springs,
rivers, and floods of love, delight, and joy. Christ
cannot tire or weary from eternity to be Christ;
and so, He must not, He cannot but be an infinite
and eternal flowing sea, to diffuse and let out
streams and floods of boundless grace. Say that
the rose were eternal; the sweet smell, the loveliness of greenness and colour must be eternal. Oh,
what a happiness, for a soul to lose its excellency
in His transcendent glory! What a blessedness
for the creature, to cast in his little all in Christ's
matchless all-sufficiency! Could all the streams
retire into the fountain and first spring, they
should be kept in a more sweet and firm possession
of their being, in the bosom of their first cause,
than in their borrowed channels that they now
move in. Our neighbourhood, and retiring in, to
dwell for ever and ever in the fountain-blessedness,
Jesus Christ, with our borrowed goodness, is the
firm and solid fruition of our eternal happy being.
Christ is the sphere, the connaturalfirst spring
and element of borrowed drops and small pieces
of created grace. The rose is surest in being, in
beauty, on its own stalk and root: let life and sap

be eternally in the stalk and root, and the rose keep its first union with the root, and it shall never wither, never cast its blossom nor greenness of beauty. It is violence for a gracious soul to be out of his stalk and root; union here is life and happiness; therefore the Church's last prayer in canonic Scripture is for union, ' Amen : Even so, come, Lord Jesus.' It shall not be well till the Father and Christ the prime heir, and all the weeping children, be under one roof in the palace royal. It is a sort of mystical lameness, that the head wanteth an arm or a finger ; and it is a violent and forced condition, for arm and finger to be separated from the head. The saints are little pieces of mystical Christ, sick of love for union. The wife of youth, that wants her husband some years, and expects he shall return to her from over-sea lands, is often on the shore ; every ship coming near shore is her new joy ; her heart loves the wind that shall bring him home. She asks at every passenger news : ' Oh ! saw ye my husband ? What is he doing ? When shall he come ? Is he shipped for a return ? ' Every ship that carrieth not her husband is the breaking of her heart. The bride the Lamb's wife, blesseth the feet of the messengers that preach such tidings, ' Rejoice, O Zion, put on thy beautiful garments, thy King

is coming.' Yea, she loveth that quarter of the
sky, that being rent asunder and cloven, shall
yield to her Husband, when He shall put through
His glorious hand, and shall come riding on the
rainbow and clouds to receive her to Himself."

After all, Rutherfurd's life and death speak
with one voice, and the central and characteristic
thing in him is also the highest. Essentially, his
life is not a theory of Christ. It is not even a
picture of Christ. It is a mere window—a
window which enabled him not so much to show
that Face to other men as before all things and
above all things to gaze upon it himself. Men
have complained that the window is colourless.
It is enough for a window that it be transparent,
provided only that there be a living face outside
˙which gives itself to be seen. The window does
not make the Face, and the Face is all that the
gazer desires.[1] It is indeed this merely transparent
and passionate intuition which gives Rutherfurd

[1] May I venture to quote a few sentences from an old
book which Rabbi John Duncan taught me to love?

"There is a certain peculiar strain, or (if I may so call
it) heroic temperament of love, which, wherever it is
found, makes it belong, as unalienable, unto God. The
very nobleness of it entitles Him to it. . . . Other passions,
like other rivers, are most liked when they calmly flow.
within their wonted banks; but of Seraphic Love, as of

his place in the Evangelical Succession of the
world, and will continue to do so, so long as men
believe that Christ is not dead who died for men.
This is that in Rutherfurd which is for all time.
Other things more for his time, and perhaps for
ours, have led us, as they led him, too far afield,
and from all of these we, like him, now come back
to that memorable close.   We come back to learn
how, during a lifelong communion with the unseen,

> "That one Face, far from vanish, rather grows,
> Or decomposes but to recompose,
> Becomes my universe that feels and knows ! "

"Life," says the same great modern poet, "is
just our chance of the prize of finding love," and
Rutherfurd's native country needs not less, but a
great deal more of this general doctrine.   But
within that generality there is one particular
suggestion with which we may close.   Rutherfurd's name seems to me fitted to remind the

Nilus, the very inundations might be desirable, and His
overflowings make Him the more welcome . . . Seraphic
love (whose passionateness is its best complexion) has
then most approached its noblest measure, when it can
least be measured.   For he alone loves God as much as he
ought, that, loving Him as much as he can, strives to repair
the deplored imperfection of that love, with an extreme
regret to find his love no greater."—*Seraphic Love:* a
Letter by the Hon. Robert Boyle.

world at large, and especially our utilitarian Scotland, that the love of God is for man the crown
and goal of all things,[1] and that religion is not a
means only, but an end. True, it is also the
greatest of all means. "No heart is pure that
is not passionate; no virtue is safe that is not
enthusiastic." Yet amid all our lifting of levers
and turning of wheels, let us remember that religion is not mere motive power, nor is it a matter
of police outward or inward. It is not mere
machinery of salvation or mere means even of
holiness; religion is its own end, and love exists
for love. And love is better than consistency,
better than good sense, better than good taste,
better than moderation, better even than wisdom.
All these are noble gifts, and they are all the gifts
of love. But love is better than all the gifts of
love.

[1] The only time I have been in Anwoth churchyard, I
found myself sitting on a stone with the date 1621, and
the inscription : "Omnia praetereunt praeter amare Deum,'
which must words presumably have been there when
Rutherfurd came to the parish.

II.

SIR GEORGE MACKENZIE.

SIR GEORGE MACKENZIE.

AMONG those persecutors of the Covenanters, whose names are mentioned " with a peculiar energy of hatred wherever the Scottish race is found on the surface of the globe," [1] the subject of our study has long held a place of especial abhorrence. " What, sir, wad ye speak to me," said Davie Deans, when a neighbour had suggested a youthful relative of Mackenzie as a suitable lawyer for poor Effie's plea, " about a man that has the blood of the saints at his fingers' ends ? Didna his eme (uncle) die and gang to his place wi' the name of the Bluidy Mackenyie? and winna he be kenned by that name sae lang as there's a Scots tongue to speak the word ? " In confirmation of this grim prophecy, we need only refer to two testimonies—one of them again from Sir Walter Scott, who by no means exaggerates the popular feeling against the memory of these men. But turn to that wonderful story in *Red-*

[1] Lord Macaulay.

gauntlet, supposed to be told so late as this century,
about the tenant who swore he would go to hell
to see his savage old laird, and suddenly found
himself in a great hall amid the ghastly revellers,
now, as of old, "birling the red wine and speaking
blasphemy and sculduddry" after a day of persecution. "There was the fierce Middleton, and the
dissolute Rothes, and the crafty Lauderdale; and
Dalzell, with his bald head and a beard to his
girdle; and Earlshall, with Cameron's blude on his
hand; and wild Bonshaw, that tied blessed Mr.
Cargill's limbs till the blood sprang; and Dun-
barton Douglas, the twice-turned traitor baith to
country and king; and Claverhouse, as beautiful
as when he lived, with his long, dark, curled locks,
streaming down over his laced buff coat;" and,
prominent among the doomed ghosts, "there was
the bluidy Advocate Mackenzie, who, for his
worldly wit and wisdom, had been to the rest as
a god." But we need not go to books, either of
fiction or history. Sir George Mackenzie's tomb
in the Greyfriars churchyard of Edinburgh, erected
by him in his lifetime, is a gloomy structure of
stone, surmounted by a ponderous cupola, and
shut in by a massive door, locked and barred.
At the present day, as for generations back, the
boys of the old town of Edinburgh (those of them

especially whose parents are connected with the
moorland districts of Scotland) hold it a feat of
daring to go to the persecutor's tomb as the
gloaming, darkens into night, and, with trembling
lips and feet prepared for instant flight, to shout
through the key-hole the quaint and horrible
adjuration—

> " Lift the sneck and draw the bar,
> Bluidy Mackenyie, come out an ye daur ! " [1]

Now who was this man, buried for centuries
under the execration of a whole people ? He was,
as a political adversary, but a wise judge and a
most candid contemporary observer,[2] confessed,
"the brightest Scotsman of his time." Even
Dryden, at the summit of his fame, avowed that
his poetic efforts and successes were originated by
the conversation of "that noble wit of Scotland,
Sir George Mackenzie." [3] He was an eminent
lawyer, in the great age of the lawyers of a nation
which was always governed by its lawyers; and
his institutional works are to this day of high
authority in the jurisprudence of Scotland. He
was not only a lawyer, but a reformer of the law,

---

[1] Anglice :—

> " Lift the latch and draw the bar,
> Bloody Mackenzie, come out if you dare."

[2] Lord Fountainhall.   [3] *Discourse on Satire*.

and he claims, with justice, that the changes in its administration which he procured were in the direction of protecting the rights of the subject and of the accused against the influence of the Crown and the Bench. Lastly, we shall be able to prove that this persecutor was anything but a bigot; that he was imbued with large and latitudinarian principles in all matters relating to religion; that these principles had the strongest influence over himself personally, and were a rule and guide in his whole public course; and, in particular, that they had the closest connection with those political measures against the Presbyterians which he originated as a minister of the Crown, or carried into execution as public prosecutor.

Sir George Mackenzie of Rosehaugh was born in 1636, a son of the Laird of Lochslin, near Tain, of the powerful family of Seaforth. In his tenth year he had become "master of his grammar and of all the common classic authors," at Dundee; in his sixteenth he had finished his studies in Greek and philosophy at Aberdeen and St. Andrews, and for three years more he read civil law at Bourges, then "the Athens of lawyers." It is unnecessary to trace his professional success and eminence. In 1661 he was already counsel

for the great Marquis of Argyll on his trial for
treason, and met the reproof of the bench for the
freedom of his defence with the bold and true
rejoinder, "That it was impossible to plead for
a traitor without speaking treason." When the
famous quarrel between the Faculty of Advocates
and the Supreme Court, before which they practised, took place, and the former, banished by
royal command from Edinburgh, emigrated to
Linlithgow, as to a *Mons Sacer* over against their
forsaken halls, Sir George, now King's Advocate,
cast in his lot with his brethren, but appeared
alone before the incensed tribunal, and successfully
urged an amnesty in an address still preserved,
concluding with the words, "Oblige in this your
native country, who miss us, as ye know ; oblige
in this your law, that needs such instruments,
especially in its infancy." From 1677 to the
Revolution, with a very short break, he was Lord
Advocate and a member of the Privy Council of
Scotland, and the year after his appointment he
published his *Laws and Customs of Scotland in
Matters Criminall*, which became the manual of
criminal law in Scotland for a hundred and thirty
years. But some parts of his legal writings have
a more general interest, and among these we may
reckon his *Idea Eloquentiæ Forensis Hodiernæ,*

and a corresponding treatise in English on *What Eloquence is fit for the Bar.* It appears that at the first institution of the Scots College of Justice it was appointed by an Act of that body (half of whom were Churchmen), that " All argunning " (which term was used in that age for arguing) " should be *syllogisticè,* and not *rhetoricè :* " a regulation against which the King's Advocate defends " the auguster and more splendid manner of debating which is now used." His arguments are not very convincing, though there is something in his advice to " my friends who *begin* to speak, first to study fluency, and when they are arrived at a consistency there, they may easily refine the large stock they have laid together." But the following passage is curious :—

" It may seem a paradox to others, but to me it appears undeniable, that the Scottish idiom of the British tongue is more fit for pleading than either the English idiom or the French tongue ; for certainly a pleader must use a brisk, smart, and quick way of speaking ; whereas the English, who are a grave nation, use a too slow and grave pronunciation, and the French a too soft and effeminate one. And, therefore, I think the English is fit for haranguing, the French for complimenting, but the Scots for pleading. Our pronunciation is like ourselves, fiery, abrupt, sprightly and bold ; their greatest wits, being employed at court, have indeed enriched very much their language as to conversation ; but all ours bending themselves to study the law, the chief science in repute with us, hath much smoothed our language as to pleading. And when I compare our law with the law of England, I perceive that our law favours more pleading than theirs does ; for their statutes and decisions are so full and authoritative, that scarce any case admits pleading, but (like an hare killed in the seat) 'tis immediately surprised by a decision or a statute."

" For my own part," says Mackenzie, in conclusion, " I pretend to no bays ; but shall think myself happy in wanting, as the fame, so the envy which attends eloquence ; and I think my own imperfections sufficiently repaid by fate, in that it has reserved me for an age wherein I heard, and daily hear, my colleagues plead so charmingly, that my pleasure does equal their honour."

And this brings us to notice, in passing, the celebrated " characteres " of some of his contemporaries by Mackenzie, with which Boswell beguiled Johnson's leisure in distant Dunvegan. Some of these are exceedingly pithy—for example, his description of the great feudal lawyer Craig, whose learning and authority made him independent of eloquence, and " trunco, non frondibus, effecit umbram ; " Hope, who when he proposed an argument or objection, " rationem addebat, et

ubi dubia videbatur, rationis rationem;" Lockhart,
that "corpus alterum juris civilis;" and young
Gilmour, "pecuniæ contemptor famæ avarus;"
the elder Gilmour, whose massive common sense,
without learning, made him seem "jura potius
ponere quam de jure respondere," and who, like
another Hercules, "nodosa et nulla arte perpolita
clava adversarios prostravit; sine rhetorica elo-
quens, sine literis doctus;" while Nisbet, the
King's Advocate immediately before Mackenzie,
had exactly the opposite qualities, so that when
Gilmour and he contended, "penes Gilmorum
gloria, penes Nisbetum palma fuit, quoniam in hoc
plus artis et cultus, in illo plus naturæ et virium."
But perhaps Mackenzie's best legal monument is
the Advocate's Library of Edinburgh, an institution over the origination of which he carefully
watched, and at whose opening, in 1689, he, as
Dean of Faculty, delivered a quaint and stately
Latin oration. It has since risen to be one of the
few great libraries in Britain; but not all who
have enjoyed its advantages have remembered to
whom they owed the opulent leisure, close to the
din of the forum, amid which we pen these lines—
"nobis hæc otia fecit." He claims for it the title
of the first existing library of law, and urges the
advantage of possessing in common, "as was the

manner in the age of gold," all the books which
could aid or illustrate that jurisprudence which
they venerate as Queen of the Sciences, from the
reported judgments of the Bench—"veras illas
et immortales judicum imagines"—up to the civil
law itself, "quod cœlo potius quam Romæ debe-
mus."

But enough of him as a lawyer. When he was
only twenty-four years old he published his
Aretina, or *Serious Romance*, "wherein he gave
a very bright specimen of a gay and exuberant
genius." This is not included in the two folio
volumes of his works which were published about
1716, but certain poems are, the chief of which,
Cœlia's Counting-House and Closet, is serious rather
than romantic, and *ennuyeux* above all. But
what Sir George valued himself upon as much as
upon any of his public acts, was his Moral Essays,
some of them written in his youth, others composed, or at least published, in his age, and giving
(the former at least) a very fair insight into the
man. One of the most artificial of these was
published in 1665—*A Moral Essay : preferring
Solitude to Public Employment, and all its Appan-
ages, such as Fame, Command, Riches, Pleasures,
Conversation, etc.* It is, as might be expected,
addressed to Celadon, quotes the seraphic Mr.

Boyle, and perhaps the best thing in it is the
motto on the title-page, which gives the response
of the Shunammite woman of quality to the question of the Hebrew courtier, "Wouldst thou be
spoken for to the king, or to the captain of the
host? And she said, I dwell among mine own
people." His biographer quaintly intimates that
this was written "in that great man's youth,
when he was free from business," and that the
dislike to public employment did not survive his
advancement, after which "his thoughts and
studies were wholly taken up in the service of his
king and country." It is quite clear, however,
that a half-stoic, half-epicurean self-restraint was
the ideal which Mackenzie had set before himself
in youth, and that this doctrine was not without
influence on his public conduct. In 1667 he published a much pithier treatise, on *Moral Gallantry;*
"a discourse—wherein the author endeavours to
prove that *point of honour* (abstracting from all
other ties) obliges men to be virtuous, and that
there is nothing so mean (or unworthy of a
gentleman) as vice." This, afterwards the argument of Steele's *Christian Hero,* fell very appropriately to the Scottish cavalier lawyer, one of
whose most careful quasi-legal works is on the
science of heraldry, which he took up because "I

found it looked upon abroad as the science of gentlemen," and the concluding sentence of which is worth quoting as the quintessence of this feeling :—

" Thus have I, for the honour and satisfaction of my country, interrupted so far the course of my ordinary studies at spare hours ; . . . . and as it is much nobler to raise a science than to be raised by it, so having writ this book as a gentleman, I design as little praise or thanks, as I would disdain all other rewards."

The Discourse on Point of Honour is dedicated to "the dissolute Rothes," with the boundless flatteries of the time ; but is preceded by an address to the nobility and gentry, in which the author claims to have "lighted this, though the smallest and dimmest of Virtue's torches, at Honour's purest flame," while in a third prefatory statement of his design, he apologises in the most curious way for his undertaking :—

" I find that it is a part of my employment, as a man and a Christian, to plead for virtue against vice ; and really, as a barrister, few subjects will employ more my invention, or better more my unlaboured eloquence, than this can do. And I find that, both by writing and speaking moral philosophy, I may contract a kindness for virtue ; seeing such as repeat a lie with almost any frequency do at last really believe it."

To the Earl of Rothes he says he designs these to be his last words in print; but they are succeeded by " A Moral Paradox, maintaining that it is much easier to be virtuous than vicious," dedicated appropriately enough to one of the honourable members of the Royal Society, and ending with the sentence " Adieu for ever to writing."   Unfortunately, however, a certain *Consolation against Calumnies* is subjoined also to this discourse, " because of the contingency of the subjects; " but this does at last come to an end, and closes with what he calls elsewhere " my beloved verse "—

" Hi motus animorum, a'que hæc certamina tanta,
Pulveris exigui jactu, compressa quiescunt."

Many years passed, and Mackenzie, after serving Charles II. and James II., and in vain defending the latter in the Scots Parliament against its downright declaration of forfeiture of the Crown, retired in dread of assassination to Oxford, and was admitted in a congregation of Regents in June, 1690, to study in the public library.   He survived only a year; but here he published one or two works which need not detain us, a *Moral History of Frugality*, dedicated to the University, and an *Essay on Reason*, which gained more reputation. It is dedicated to the Hon. Robert Boyle, "as a token of our friendship," and immediately on its being published at London in 1690, attracted the attention of the learned Grævius, who "put a preface to it," and published it in Latin at Utrecht the same year, under this title, *De Humanæ Rationis Imbecillitate.* There is nothing very striking in it, however, except some sentiments on bigotry, which we shall presently notice, and a spirited argument in defence of the position, "I know no greater enemy to just thought or reasoning than raillery and satyrs, and the new way of reasoning, ridiculous similies." There is, he grants, a justice in "scourging, defaming, and banishing vice; and this jurisdiction is given by heaven immediately to such as have sense." But wit is a salt, and should be used "plentifully in conversation, moderately in business, but never in religion," the use of it there having, he thinks, a close connection with bigotry. It may be feared that Sir George, in his last years, safe in the peaceful halls of Oxford from the distant execration of his Whig and Presbyterian foes, was more sensitive to the few personal sarcasms which penetrated his retreat than to the reasonings or the wrath, both of which he had always been ready to confront.

But by far the ablest of Mackenzie's books, and the one also which throws most light on his private sentiments and public career, is his *Religio Stoici*, published in 1663, and finished before his twenty-eighth year. The title reminds one of Sir Thomas Browne; and not the title alone. The quaintness of the first words, " Albeit man be but a statue of dust kneaded with tears, moved by the hidden engines of his restless passions," suggests an inferior imitation of the same model, and no one who has ever reverentially studied the *Hydrio-taphia* or the *Religio Medici* can be at a loss to know whom the following sentences by Sir George recall :—

" That brain hath too little *pia mater*, that is, too curious to know, why God, who evidences so great a desire to save poor man, did yet suffer him to fall."

" Albeit the glass of my years hath not yet turned five-and-twenty, yet the curiosity I have to know the different limbos of departed souls, and to view the card of the region of death, would give me abundance of courage to encounter this king of terrors, though I were a Pagan ; but when I consider what joys are prepared for them that fear the Almighty, and what craziness attends such as sleep in Methusalem's cradle, I pity them who make long life one of the oftest repeated petitions of their Pater Noster."

The author's design in this discourse he states to be "this one principle, that speculations in religion are not so necessary, and are more dangerous than sincere practice. *It is in religion, as in heraldry, the simpler the bearing be, it is so much the purer and the ancienter.*" The sentiment of this admirable comparison he expounds throughout his treatise, and particularly in *The Stoic's Friendly Address to the Fanatics of all Sects and Sorts*, which precedes the treatise itself.

"I am none of those who acknowledge no temples, besides those of their own heads. And I am of opinion that such as think they have a church within their own breasts, should likewise believe their heads are steeples, and so should *provide them with bells.* I believe that there is a Church militant, which, like the ark, must lodge in its bowels all such as are to be saved from the flood of condemnation : but to chalk out its bordering lines, is beyond the geography of my religion. He was infallible who compared God's spirit to the wind that bloweth where it listeth : we hear the sound of it, but know not whence it comes or whither it goeth. And the name graven on the white stone none knows but he who hath it."

"Most of all Christians," he says in his chapter of the strictness of churches, "do, like coy maids, lace their bodies so strait that they bring on them a consumption ; " but—

"Since discretion opened my eyes, I have always judged it necessary for a Christian to look oftener to his practice of piety than to confession of faith ; and to fear more the crookedness of his will, than the blindness of his judgment ; delighting more to walk on from grace to grace, thus working out the work of his own salvation with fear and trembling, than to stand still with the Galileans, curiously gazing up into heaven."

Few writers are more severe than he whom his countrymen have called "the bloody Mackenzie" against all persecution for the sake of truth ; nor can there be any doubt of his sincerity in this.

"Opinion," he argues, "kept within its own proper bounds, is a pure act of the mind; and so it would appear that to punish the body for that which is a sin of the soul, is as unjust as to punish one relation for another. . . . Matters of religion and faith resemble some curious pictures and optic prisms, which seem to change shapes and colours, according to the several stances from which the aspicient views them. . . . God (who loves us all infinitely better than any one of us doth another) leaves us, upon our own hazard, a freedom in our choice ; albeit we poor miscreants compel each other, denying to our fellow-creatures that freedom which He allows all the creation."

A few of these sentences almost remind one of the more sceptical utterances of the school of Hobbes ; but, as a general rule, Mackenzie is quite orthodox. It is not so much the positions he adopts, as the tone of the whole, that makes it clear to the reader that there was not very much earnestness in the matter, and, in particular, not much earnestness about truth. The "stoical indolency" which he admires and claims, is certainly here along with Christian charity ; and the other title which he gives to his book, *The Virtuoso* in religion, hits off exactly its freedom from that personal subjection to truth, that absolute obligation to obey it in all its details, which characterised the other or Puritan side. The whole legislation of Mackenzie's country since the Reformation, is dominated by the absolute authority which it ascribed to religious truth, and by the assumption that a body or organic whole of truth can be found in Scripture—two positions which our lawyer avoids admitting, but does not attempt to deny. But, he says—

" Albeit the knowledge and acknowledgment of a God be the basis of true Stoicism, and a firmer one than any the heathens could pretend to, yet that knowledge of Him which, by the curiosity of schoolmen, and the bigotry of tub preachers, is now formed in a body of Divinity, is of all others the least necessary and the most dangerous ; "

and that, as he goes on to explain, not because

the existing theology was false or mischievous,
but because theology itself is a superfluous thing
for the people in general, and for the pulpit. The
pulpit, of course, in the country of Knox, was
Mackenzie's greatest enemy; and his speculations
upon it are quite prophetic of that severe legislation of which he was afterwards the chief
promoter.·

"Nothing hath more busied my thoughts than to
find a reason why the heathens, who were as assiduous,
and zealous too, in the worship of their gods as we
Christians, did never frequent sermons, nor know no
such part·of Divine service ; whereof probably the
reason was because their governors (whose commands
amongst them were the sole *jure-divino-ship* of all
ecclesiastical rites) feared that Churchmen, if they had
been licensed to harangue to the people, would have
influenced too much that gross body ; which was the
reason likewise why, in the Primitive Church (as one
of their historians observes), *ex formula populo prædi-
cabant, tantum antiquitas timebat* δημογωγους. ' They
preached only approved sermons, so much did antiquity
fear those leaders of the people '—a practice, it is
reported, lately renewed by the Duke of Russia. And
this seemeth also to have been the reason why all
liturgies have picked texts for their preachers, lest, if
they had been left a freedom in their choice, they had
chose such as might in the letter have suited best with
such seditious libels as are now obtruded on the

people, in lieu of pious homilies, at remarkable or festive occasions."

That political considerations such as these had much to do with the Conventicle Acts, and other detestable statutes of the time in Scotland, there can be no doubt, any more than there can be of the frequent turbulence and violence of the pulpit. But it is still more instructive to trace the deeper ground of opposition between the two schools. It was no mere contrast between dogmatism and individualism. Then, as afterwards, the pulpit was the chief organon by which the rugged-minded peasantry of Scotland were taught to think; but even this characteristic was distasteful to those now rising into power.

" Among all the innovations introduced by our infant divines, I hate none more than that of giving reasons for proving the doctrine, which being Scripture itself, can be proved by nothing that is more certain. As for instance, where the doctrine is, *that God loved us freely*, how can this be proved more convincingly than thus, *my text says it*? And that is *idem per idem*, a most unlogical kind of probation. When I then go to church, I should love to spend my time in praises and prayers "—

in which also, unfortunately, the Presbyterians show an unnecessary earnestness and length, and

6

"screech like Baal's priests, as if God were no nearer to them than the visible heavens."

A religious stoic is not necessarily much of a Churchman, and a religious virtuoso may be very little of one. But the road which Sir George Mackenzie took to being so is a very intelligible one.

" I have travelled no further in theology than a Sabbath-day's journey, and, therefore, it were arrogance in me to offer a map of it to the credulous world. But if I were worthy to be consulted in these spiritual securities, I should advise every private Christian rather to stay still in the barge of the Church, with the other disciples, than by an ill-bridled zeal to hazard drowning alone with Peter, by offering to walk upon the unstable surface of his own fleeting and water-weak fancies, though with a pious resolution to meet our Saviour."

And the very next sentence shows that the position thus taken by our author differs *toto cœlo* from that originally held by all the Reformed Churches, and emphatically by his own stubborn countrymen. Scotland has always been an ecclesiastical country, and rather an intolerant one; yet, age after age, nothing there draws down deeper contempt and condemnation than the renouncing or suppressing of individual opinion in order to conform to a Church majority or creed. In

Mackenzie's time, and before it, many a man must have done this; but no one ever confessed it, or regarded the imputation as other than one of scoundrelism. The following utterance by Sir George Mackenzie would have made Knox and his compeers turn in their graves, could they have read it :—

"Albeit, one may be a real Christian, and yet differ from the Church, which says, that the wise men who came to bow before our Saviour's cradle-throne were three kings, and in such other opinions as these wherein the fundamentals of faith and quiet of the Church are no ways concerned ; yet certainly he were no wise man himself, nor yet sound Christian, who would not, even in these, bow the flag of his private opinion to the commands of the Church. The Church is our mother, and therefore we should wed no opinion without her consent who is our parent ; or if we have rashly wedded any, it is in the power of the Church and her officials to grant us a divorce."

Twenty years of the boot and gallows could not make the opposition of Scotland to these doctrines more deadly and irreconcilable than it was when they were first uttered. At the same time it is quite clear from them that Mackenzie's aversion to persecution *for the sake of truth* was abundantly sincere. What is not as yet equally clear is,

whether he was opposed to persecution *for the sake
of conformity.*

But other passages in the *Religious Stoic* leave
no doubt on this point, and they are by far the
most important in a historical point of view.
Thus in an interesting passage on the variety of
opinions in Churches :—

"It is remarkable, that albeit infallibility be not by all
conceded to any militant Church, yet it is assumed by
all ; neither is there any Church under the sun which
would not fix the name of heretic, and account him
(almost) reprobate, who would refuse to acknowledge
the least rational of their principles ; and thus these
Churchmen pull up the ladders from the reach of
others, after they have scaled the walls of preferment
themselves. . . . The fanatic believes the Lord's
Supper but a ceremony, though taken with very little
outward respect ; the Presbyterian allows it, but will
not kneel; the Episcopist kneels, but will not adore
it ; the Catholic mixeth adoration with his kneeling.
And thus most of all religions are made up of the
same elements, albeit their asymbolic qualities pre-
domine in some more than in others. And if that
maxim hold, that *majus et minus non variant speciem,*
we may pronounce all of them to be one religion.

"The Church, like the river Nilus, can hardly condescend where its head lies, and as all condescend that
the Church is a multitude of Christians, so join all
their opinions, and you shall find that they will have
it to have, like the multitude, many heads. *But in*

*this, as in all articles not absolutely necessary for being
saved, I make the laws of my country to be my creed."*

This is perhaps the most significant statement
in the treatise, and it is not surprising to find the
author start a little at the sound he has made,
and in the following "Postscript" to the last
chapter attempt to explain it away into ambiguity.

"By the *laws of this country* the author means that
religion which is settled by law. In other respects
the author recommends himself to the gloss of the
reader's charity."

This explanation—the only touch of positive
disingenuousness in this able tractate—was of
course useless to mitigate the condemnation which
the original proposition drew down. There has
never been a time in Scotland in which even the
amended proposition, that in matters of less importance "I make the religion settled by law *to be
my creed,"* would not be received with some loathing
and indignation. The other formula, "I make
the laws of my country to be my creed," is a little
more naked and offensive in expression; but the
moral objection to both is precisely the same, and
the putting into express propositions the suggestions already made (of suppressing or dissembling
personal belief at the bidding of authority) fixed a

gulf as deep as hell between this youthful Scotsman, the brightest of his time, and the mass of
his countrymen. The real importance of the
phrase about "the laws of my country" was that
the men in the court of Charles II., who were
beginning to use such phrases, and who honestly
hated persecuting either themselves or others for
the sake of truth, were now in power. And there
was just such a chance that, with all their indifference to truth, they might be disposed to
make the laws of their country the creed not only
of themselves, but of their unfortunate fellow-
subjects.

We have already seen that Mackenzie depre-
cates persecution for the sake of dogma. In the
Stoic's Address to the Fanatics he points out with
much wit the *uselessness* of this way of compelling
others for their good—yet here too there is a most
ominous postscript,

"I am apt to believe that, if laws and lawgivers did
not make heretics vain, by taking too much notice of
their extravagances, the world should be no more
troubled with these than they are with the chimeras
of alchymists and philosophers. And it fares with
them, as with tops, which, how long they are scourged,
keep foot and run pleasantly, but fall how soon they
are neglected and left to themselves. . . . *Albeit, I
confess, when these not only recede from the canonized*

*creed of the Church, but likewise encroach upon the laws
of the State, then, as of all others they are the most
dangerous, so of all others they should be most severely
punished."*

A man who has defined a heretic as one whose
opinions may be not only sincere *but true*, but who
will not suppress them in favour of the religion
settled by law, and who follows this up by a
declaration that such heretics should be most
severely punished ; a Lord Advocate who, thirteen
years before taking office, has published such a
declaration—such a man has already sown the
seeds of what the unimpassioned Hallam calls the
" thirty infamous years that completed the mis-
fortunes and degradation of Scotland."[1] And it
appears to me that a great characteristic of the
religious oppressions of which Charles II.'s Advocate has always been held the mainspring, has
been somewhat overlooked. Up to this time there
had been persecutions in Scotland, for the sake of
religion, on both sides. But they were, or professed to be, persecutions for the sake of truth,
and the most sacred of all names was abused by
the sword and the axe being used in its defence.

[1] "No part, I believe, of modern history, for so long a
period, can be compared for the wickedness of government
to the Scots Administration of this reign."—*Constitutional
History of England*, ch. xvii.

Now for the first time there was risk of a religious
state tyranny, in which the actors had no belief
in the religion which they forced upon others.
And it remained to be seen whether the intolerance of indifference would be more tolerable than
the intolerance of conscience.

Sir George Mackenzie long afterwards published
a *Vindication of the Government in Scotland*, the
comparison of which with his early Stoical Essay
is invaluable. The Vindication opens with the
statement, that " the civil government in Scotland was never bigot in that king's reign,"
and on that account he thinks it unnecessary to
consider either Episcopacy or Presbytery in themselves, neither of them having been held to be
Jure Divino. I am inclined to think that the
claim he here puts forward is a true one; nor
perhaps is the other assertion which he goes on to
make false, that " the governors for the time can
truly and boldly say that no man in Scotland ever
suffered for his religion." It was not of religious
opinions entertained in secret that the Government was afraid, it was the honest and open
profession of them that it sought to crush.
Mackenzie, indeed, had put the thing exceedingly
well in his early treatise (*Stoic's Address to the
Fanatics*) :—

"As every private Christian should be tolerated by his fellow-subjects *to worship God inwardly* according to his conscience, so should all conspire in that exterior *uniformity of worship* which the laws of his country enjoin. . . . That traveller were absurd who would rather squabble with those among whom he sojourns, than observe those rites and customs which are required by the laws of the places where he lives."

Of course, to persecute for inward opinion, or worshipping inwardly, is a pure impossibility. No man can do it, and no man ever tried to do it. All that can be done by the most relentless is to insist on *outward* dissembling of belief, or suppression of belief, or "exterior uniformity of worship," and if this is enjoined by the laws, and failure in it punished by them, it matters little whether the State is bigot enough to believe in the sacredness of the worship it commands, or lax enough to hold it sacred only because it is commanded. Which of these was the case in Scotland during the evil days of the last two Stuarts? On this point we shall call no other witness than the official apologist of the Government itself, in the carefully composed Vindication which he printed after the Revolution of 1688.

After the Restoration, he says, "the Parliament of Scotland being called, enquired very

seriously into the occasion of such disorders"
(those during the Commonwealth), "and soon
found that they were all to be charged upon the
Solemn League and Covenant, and those who
adhered thereto"—those who signed it including
most of the members of the Parliament itself, as
well as the king—"and therefore they endea-
voured to persuade the Presbyterians to disown
the Covenant, all favour being promised to them
on that condition."

"But finding that the Presbyterians generally
thought themselves bound to own the Covenant, the
Parliament, concluding that the same men, owning the
same principles, would be ready upon occasion to act
over the same things, *therefore* they, by vote (which
may be called unanimous, seeing only four or five
dissented), *restored Episcopacy,* and that so much the
rather because *that government* had in no age nor place
forced its way into the State by the sword, *but had
still been brought in by the uncontroverted magistrate,*
without ever thrusting itself in by violence. *And yet
the Government did sustain Episcopacy as a part of
the State, but never as a hierarchy wholly independent
from it.*"

He goes on to tell how, the Presbyterians still
frequenting their conventicles, the State forbade
all above five to meet at worship in a house; and
when they, to evade this, met in the open air, the

State forbade this also, ultimately under the
penalty of death—all carrying out the "exterior
uniformity of worship " which is lawful for a State
to enforce, while respecting the free exercise of
conscience in the individual heart or the private
family. We might leave it to constitutional
historians to criticise the very disreputable transaction glossed over in the paragraph last quoted :
all that it is necessary now to point out is that
Episcopacy was confessedly brought in as a piece
of State machinery, and not as a matter of conscience.[1] Sir George Mackenzie indicates this,
and he may be very fully believed. Had it been
a question as to Charles I. and Laud, there might
be more doubt. But neither Charles II. nor the
set of singularly unprincipled men who formed his
Privy Council in Scotland—Mackenzie in some
ways the most respectable of them all—need be
supposed to have cared more upon the subject

[1] The doctrine of the Episcopal was identical with that
of the Presbyterian Church. Even "the way of worship
in our Church," as Mackenzie says in his Vindication,
" differed nothing from what the Presbyterians themselves
practised (except only, that we used the Doxology, the
Lord's Prayer, and in Baptism the Creed, all of which they
rejected) ; we had no ceremonies, surplice, altars, or cross
in baptism." The change was made purely for the purpose
of subordinating and overruling the Church.

than they professed to do. A religion which
could be "brought in by the magistrate," and
which could be patronised by men in power as
"part of the State," but without their accept-
ing any burden of duty or conscience from it, was
in every way the best for them. And we have
now a very curious confirmation, in a private
document of Mackenzie's, of the real nature of the
transaction which we have spoken of as disreputable to all the parties concerned. Long after our
author's death, in the year of the present century
1821, an old MS., rescued by Dr. McCrie from a
grocer's shop in Edinburgh, was found to give an
account by him of the strange scene in London in
which the second Charles was persuaded by his
councillors to violate his recent coronation promise
to maintain Presbytery. At that meeting the
nobles were all present whose names Sir Walter
has given us in the denunciation of Wandering
Willie—"the fierce Middleton, and the dissolute
Rothes, and the crafty Lauderdale;" but the proceedings of the council were really guided by the
famous chancellor and historian, Clarendon. He
spoke first through the Earl of Middleton. "It
is arbitrary to your Majesty," said the Earl, "to
choose what government (of the Church) you will
fix there (in Scotland); for to your Majesty this

is, by the last Act of Supremacy, declared to belong." Mackenzie no doubt points out that this whole London transaction was a contest between two courtiers—Middleton and Lauderdale—as to which could best gain royal favour by sacrificing the views of the Scottish people; six-sevenths of whom, as the Earl of Crawford told the king at that very meeting, were against the proposed change. But that was the very reason why the change was made. As Sir George puts it, it was because the " Presbyterians generally " went in the other direction that " the Parliament restored Episcopacy," and that as " a part of the state."

Besides, we are not left to Mackenzie's testimony, public and private. The statute itself, " Restoring the ancient order of bishops," frankly takes the bull by the horns, and attacks in its preamble that Church independence which the Presbyterians held sacred. There is no pretence of referring the question to the Church itself. On the contrary, " Forasmuch as the ordering and disposal of the external government and policy of the Church doth properly belong unto his Majestie, as an inherent right of the Crown, by virtue of his royal prerogative and supremacy in causes ecclesiastical," therefore, " in discharge of this trust," the change is ordered. No one

knew better than Mackenzie that the Presbyterians held organic changes made in the Church
by external authority to be unlawful, or indeed to
be null and void; and held the Church's liberty
in this respect to have been repeatedly recognised
in Scotland by Acts of Parliament. On this last
point the enactment itself is conclusive, for it goes
on to "Rescind, cass, and annull all Acts of
Parliament by which the sole and only power and
jurisdiction within this Church doth stand in the
Church, and in the general, provincial, and Pres-
byterial assemblies and kirk-sessions; and all
Acts of Parliament or Council which may be
interpreted to have given any Church power,
jurisdiction, or government to the office-bearers of
the Church, or their respective meetings, other
than that which acknowledgeth a dependance.
upon, and subordination to, the sovereign power
of the King as supreme." And the first statute
of Charles's second Parliament was devoted to a
formal reasserting of the royal supremacy over
the Church. No conception can be formed of the
systematic and deliberate tyranny of the time
ensuing, unless we advert to this statutory foundation of all the acts of administration. It was a
cruel thing to force multitudes of Scotch peasants
who were weak enough, as Mackenzie asserts, to

believe in the *Jus Divinum* of Presbytery, into
conformity against their conscience, and to do it
by fines and executions. But even those Scotsmen who might not believe in the *Jus Divinum* of
either form, believed earnestly in the sole right
and duty of the Church itself to choose the form.
Consequently, most of them held conformity to the
new system to be sinful, not merely because of
any odiousness of that system itself, but because
also of the unlawful authority by which it was
imposed. But this was the very bribe by which
the Scots Privy Council was induced to impose
it. They introduced the system, not although it
was tyrannical to do so, but *because* it was tyrannical. Of course, Episcopacy is in its own nature
no more tyrannical than Presbytery; and in
practice it has on some sides been often found to
be less so. But on this occasion in history it was
introduced by the civil power as a "part of the
State," with no statutory pretence of consulting
either the Church or the people, and with the
scarcely disguised purpose of thus bringing the
exercise of private judgment in Church matters
under the edge of the civil and criminal law.

And this was but the first step. Mackenzie,
though he privately explains and publicly defends
it, had probably less to do with it than with the

subsequent legislation. There can be no doubt
that he was connected with the Acts of Parliament on the subject of religion which crowd the
statute-book from this date, not only as the King's
Advocate who enforced, but as the draughtsman
who prepared, or at least as one of the council
who passed them. The "Bloody Advocate" has
been hitherto hated as the too-willing tool of the
arbitrary Government he served. I shall afterwards give some reasons for thinking that he may
have been harshly judged in this respect. But
it has been forgotten that he was probably the
contriver, as well as the administrator, of these
infamous measures; and that in a far more
responsible way than is now admitted to have
been the case also with Claverhouse. He was so,
we cannot doubt, on the same ground of latitudinarianism and hatred of the bigotry of private
judgment. Thus, shortly after the bishops were
appointed, the Presbyterian ministers already
ordained were ordered to seek institution at their
hands. Three or four hundred left their manses,
rather than thus deny their previous vocation, and
the country was filled with mourning and dismay.
The outed men were forbidden at once to preach
under penalties of "sedition." The people were
forbidden to hear them. Men, whose character

and attainments are described by their own
bishops as generally contemptible, hastily succeeded them; and more laws were passed forcing
the people to come to their churches. The people
refused; and were fined ruinously, and dragoons
quartered upon them till the fines were paid. It
was made incumbent upon all, under pain of
banishment or imprisonment, to reveal whom they
had seen at a conventicle. Abjuration, not only
of the Covenant, but of the independence of the
Church in ecclesiastical causes, was demanded of
all under severe penalties. Every curate was
ordered by statute to keep a list of non-con-
formists; every sheriff and county to proceed
severely against the names in the list under pain
of heavy fines. Fines, imprisonment, and exile
were denounced for having a child baptized by
an outed minister, or for being absent for three
Sundays from the parish church. And, lastly, to
preach at a conventicle in the open fields was
made *death*, with confiscation of goods.

Now all this network of horror, the results of
which quicken into passion the blood of the most
cold-hearted historians of the period, was, we have
no doubt, originally woven—was certainly thereafter held and tightened round the heart of Scotland for twenty or thirty dismal years—by the

"virtuoso," or religious stoic, whose large-minded
and liberal *Address to the Fanatics*, written in his
twenty-fourth year, we have already quoted.
Private men, he held, should yield up their
opinions on minor matters, both to the Church
and to the State ; and though dissenters from the
creed might be let alone, those who did not yield
to the law should be severely punished.   All that
remained was to *make* the law such, that those
who did not abjure their native opinions and
practices should be caught and crushed by it.
And this was done promptly, systematically, and
increasingly, until, in 1681, the *Act anent Religion
and the Test* pointed out, with perfect justice, that
the only thing that could give confidence to
" schismatical dissenters from the Established
Church " was " supine neglect of putting in execution the good laws provided against them."

Sir George Mackenzie provided the good laws :
Turner, Dalziel, and Claverhouse, with their
brutal soldiery, enforced them in the villages
where they were quartered, and in the field ; but
the final consummation in council chamber and
justiciary came round to Mackenzie again.   And
it is from his official position as public prosecutor
or informer, and from the tragical scenes in which
he was thus called upon frequently to take part,

that the bloody mark has come to be affixed to his name. I have already intimated a doubt whether this condemnation can be sustained to the extent that is popularly supposed. Sir George Mackenzie's writings show that steady and discriminating love of justice which every great lawyer possesses, if not as an original passion, at least as a slowly acquired and deep-founded habit. Not even his famous chapter on witches is an exception to this; for though it begins, " That there are witches, divines cannot doubt, seeing that the word of God hath ordained that no witch shall live, nor lawyers in Scotland, seeing our law ordains it to be punished with death," it goes on to argue that " from the horridness of this crime I do conclude, that of all crimes it requires the clearest relevancy and most convincing probation ; and I condemn, next to the witches themselves, those cruel and too forward judges, who burn persons by thousands as guilty of this crime." And as an administrator of criminal justice generally, Sir George Mackenzie seems to have merited well of his country. Before his time the accused never knew what witnesses the Crown was to bring against him ; he procured a law that a list should be furnished to the prisoner fifteen days before trial. Of old the King's Advocate (strange

to say) had the naming of the jury; Sir George
got an Act passed by which it was transferred
to the judges to select forty-five men, out of
which the defendant chose fifteen, to try the case.
In all Scots criminal cases the King's Advocate,
when prosecuting, was the last speaker, till Sir
George established the existing practice, by which
the defendant has the last word, " because ordinarily the greatest impression is supposed to be
made by the last pleading." And, finally, the
clerk of the court, appointed by the Crown, used
always to be enclosed with the jury for their
direction, till Charles II.'s law-officer got an Act
empowering them to choose their own clerk. Sir
George claims to have been the originator of all
these changes in favour of the liberty of the
subject, and we see no reason to doubt that they
were prompted by him from a pure regard to
abstract justice—as he puts it himself elsewhere,
" to oppose arbitrariness, where it is most dread-
ful, and that is in matters criminal." And such
accomplished facts must weigh more with us
than his advocacy of the abolition of jury trial,
and may even balance the unpleasant stories
which tradition preserves of him—that occasional
passion and browbeating of juries of which even
Fountainhall complains, and the darker tragedies

of Mitchell and the Earl of Argyll, in which the law seems to have been stretched, if not wrested, to bring Presbyterians accused of crime to torture or death.

The truth seems to be, that Mackenzie was not originally an unjust man, but he was an admirer of despotism, and had a hatred of private judgment; and he was engaged in a contest with a nation which was getting wearied of the former, and was determined to have the latter. Too much uprightness must not be exacted from a man who tells James II. that "Heaven only was governed by a better King" than his father, and that Scotland "cannot boast of a rich soil, or a warm sun; but it may, that it hath given these happy islands those gracious and glorious kings," the three Stuarts. We may read and admire that fine dedication of Mackenzie's great work on criminal law to the Duke of Lauderdale—

"The greatest statesman in Europe, who is a scholar; and the greatest scholar, who is a statesman; for, to hear you talk of books, one would think you had bestowed no time in studying men; and yet, to observe your wise conduct in affairs, one might be induced to believe that you had no time to study books, . . . who spend one-half of the day in studying what is just, and the other half in practising what is so."

But it is well to remember as to the nobleman

addressed, that while he had not only signed the
Covenant, but had of old been the representative
of the Scottish Kirk at the Westminster Assembly,
it was this same Duke of Lauderdale who at a
later date is said to have "made bare his arm,
and sworn by Jehovah" (at the council-table
where Mackenzie sat) that he would crush the
Westland shires into submission to Episcopacy
by even greater severities, if need be, than those
under which they groaned at the time. And the
praise Sir George Mackenzie ascribes to the trucu-
lent president of the Council may to some extent
be his own apology, that "you continue no longer
your unkindness to any man, than you think he
continues his opposition to his prince." I fear,
indeed, it must be conceded that Mackenzie's character did not improve as his official life went on.
The very last account we have of his conversation
(after its close), when Evelyn met him at the table
of the Bishop of St. Asaph's on March 9th, 1691, is
not reassuring. It was all right that the exiled
Scotsman should bear witness to "the exceeding
tyranny of those bigots who acknowledge no
superior on earth, in civil or divine matters,
maintaining that the people only have the right
of government." But his account of the origin of
Presbytery can scarcely be called ingenuous. It

was introduced, he would have his too credulous
after-dinner friends believe, by the Jesuits' Order
about the twentieth (year) of Queen Elizabeth,
"a famous Jesuit among them feigning himself
a Protestant, and bringing in that which they
since called, and are still so fond of, praying by
the spirit. This Jesuit," he added, "remained
many years before he was discovered; afterwards
died in Scotland, where he was buried at (a place
unnamed), having yet on his monument, *Rosa
Inter Spinas.*" With all allowances for one who
had himself been a rose among our thorns, this sort
of talk cannot be said to have been very kindly,
or even, as coming from a well-read lawyer, very
honest. The fact is, Mackenzie had lived amid
a bad set of men; he was hand and glove with
them; and he prospered, all his life through, in
their prosperity. It was a disadvantage, morally,
to be "the despot's champion," in an age when
civil freedom had appealed to the conscience of
our country; and it was still more so, perhaps, to
be the friend of the despot's tools. Yet I continue
to think that the central and most corrupting
influence of all—the worm at the core of
Mackenzie's whole public life—was the principle
which, as we have seen, he adopted very early,
and which he was enabled so long to illustrate at

the expense of his countrymen. For so it came to
pass that the young Scotsman, who in his assumed
character of "the Stoic" had, while not yet in
office, written to his countrymen, "My heart
bleeds when I consider how scaffolds were dyed
with Christian blood, and the fields covered with
the carcases of murdered Christians"—so it
happened that the same man has become asso-
ciated in the minds of his countrymen with
religious persecution beyond all others in the past,
with the single exception of Grahame of Claverhouse. Nor is it strange that so it should be.
For on the opposite page of the same *Address to
the Fanatics* of his time, and in the course of the
same exhortation to peace and against bigotry, we
find grim and significant allusions :—

"May not one, who is convinced in his judgment
that monarchy is the best of Governments, live
happily in Venice or Holland? And that traveller
were absurd who would rather squabble with those
among whom he sojourns, than observe those rites
and customs which are required by the laws of the
places where he lives. What is once statuted by a
law we all consent to, in choosing commissioners to
represent us in those parliaments where the laws are
made ; *and so, if they ordain us to be decimated*, or to
leave the nation if we conform not, *we cannot say when
that law is put to execution, that we are oppressed.*"

It is the true tone of despotism, and, apart from religion, it could not be acceptable in a country which produced Buchanan's *De Jure Regni*, and Rutherfurd's *Lex Rex*. Nor is the Hobbes-like theory much improved by the allusion to representation in a Parliament; the essence of the fallacy being that the subject in Scotland is supposed to have given up to the supreme power '(king or Parliament it matters not) all his original rights, even to decimation. Yet Scotland, slow and late in the growth of its civil liberties, would scarcely, as yet, have resented with so much animosity Mackenzie's mere sycophancy and proneness to despotism. What doomed the one to thirty years of misery, and the other to an ´immortal hatred, was the application of his theory to matters of conscience and religion. This lesson at least, that matters of conscience have not been given up to the civil power, whether that power be Parliament or king, Scotland had already learned; and to Scotland this became, quite otherwise than in England, the root of all subsequent attainments. Now against this doctrine Mackenzie had stead-fastly set himself, and therein he set himself against the highest aspirations of his country. No doubt the men who were most irreconcilably opposed to him were quite willing to entrust to

the Church too much of that authoritative and
persecuting power which they earnestly denied to
the State. But, strange as it may seem, they
found in this distinction a rest for conscience and
a hold on freedom and truth. It is not hard to
understand. All over Europe the original distinction between Church and State was founded in
this very claim of freedom of conscience.[1] And
while the old Scotch thought, quite rightly, that
in maintaining the freedom of the Church they
were doing battle for freedom of conscience, they
also thought, wrongly but naturally, that this was
doing *enough* for it. But their quarrel against
the whole State interference was clear and good,
and the interference at this time threatened was
considerably worse than what they had previously
dealt with. For it was now plain that if the
State was to meddle with their religion, it was to
do so in the way, not of believing it, but of merely
patronising it. A religion was to be set up and
established, and conformity was to be enacted by
force; but at the same time it was significantly
enough intimated to the nation that if they conformed externally they might do as they pleased
about inward belief. And for Sir George
Mackenzie it was reserved, after having made that

[1] See Guizot's *History of Civilization in Europe.*

hateful suggestion in the theoretical writings of
his youth, to carry it out in manhood through
years of dark laws and relentless administration.
Plainly, this able man fell upon evil days, and
was unfortunate in the country of his birth. He
was no bigot. Better for him almost if he had
been. He would at least have escaped the bitter
contempt of his own generation for one who made
the laws of his country his creed, and the infinite
hatred which still pursues the unhappy ghost that
sought to force a creedless creed on others.

But in the meantime we seem to have ascertained one fact of considerable interest. "The
persecuting times," as they were popularly called
in Scotland, were due to the same influences which
caused what are known in Church history as The
Persecutions *par excellence.* The tolerant character of the great Roman power, so far at least
as regards any real belief in the religions with
which it had to deal, is now pretty well understood. It is acknowledged on all hands that the
great Aurelius and Antonine enforced the old
religion only "as a part of the State"[1] (to use
Mackenzie's words), and that the resulting perse-

---

[1] " La seule chose à laquelle l'empire romain ait déclaré
la guerre, en fait de religion, c'est la théocratie. . . . Il
n'admettait aucune association dans l'Etat en dehors de

cutions were due purely to that intolerance of
falsehood and false profession which the new faith
inspired in its children. It was precisely so in
Scotland in "the killing time." It was not
Episcopacy that was in fault, as the Scottish
peasantry naturally believed. It was the resolve
to establish State supremacy in religious matters,
and to make the people conform in things which
the Government proclaimed to be indifferent.
Claverhouse was the too zealous minister of a
State latitudinarianism, and the Bloody Mackenzie
was a religious stoic.

　But let us, in conclusion, remember that the
false principle of his life was not Mackenzie's
alone ; it was part of the general reaction of his
age from the intense individualism of the great
Reformation impulse. Even an intellect like
Spinoza's could, in that time, bring itself, while
advocating extreme freedom of thought, to advocate also deliberate dissimulation in conformity to
the religious rule of the magistrate. But a nearer
parallel to Mackenzie is to be found nearer home ;
and I do not mean an extreme man like Hobbes.
Their great contemporary, Bishop Jeremy Taylor,

l'Etat. Ce dernier point est essentiel : il est, à vrai dire,
la racine de toutes les persécutions. '— RENAN'S *Les
Apôtres.* 1866.

had in 1647 published *The Liberty of Prophesying*
—an eloquent plea for freedom of religious opinion.
Yet in it, like Sir George, he reserved a right in
the State to enforce external conformity; and
in a subsequent volume (his *Ductor Dubitantium*,
published about the same time with the *Religio
Stoici*) he gives the king a right of legislation
and jurisdiction, even in spiritual matters. That
king was Charles II., and the exceptions thus
admitted practically nullified, for England as for
Scotland, the whole plea of religious liberty. Nor
is this all. Dr. Taylor's charming and almost
epoch-making book is tainted throughout by one
faint suggestion—that to enable men even to
tolerate maintainers of falsehood, we should not
ourselves be very certain of truth, or very earnest
to propagate it; and that if we could have full
belief in dogma, we might be, not perhaps justified,
but certainly excused, in persecuting for its sake.
The odour of that fly in his ointment has floated
down far beyond the days when Taylor became
a bishop. It clings to our literature to this hour.
The same view has been formulated into a theory
by one of the hardest intellects of our own age;
and it recurs in English historical works of the
present century with a frequency which, when
we compare with them the tone on the same

subject of continental productions of equal rank,
is undoubtedly humiliating.

But in order to say all that has to be said for
Mackenzie, we must remember the attitude, not
of his friends only, but of his adversaries. The
Presbyterians also held that the State ought to
demand of its subjects attendance upon the Church
which it provided for them; and representative
men on their side, like Samuel Rutherfurd, preached
and published and voted with the majority of the
Westminster assembly against all toleration; or,
as they more explicitly put it, against " the toleration of sects." Which of the two sides was in
theory the more intolerant may be a question.
For the Cavalier party, besides being the party
of authority in religion, always leaned to the
exercise of arbitrary power in Church matters as
in others. The Puritan party, on the other hand,
was determined to restrain the magistrate's power
by constitutional bounds; but within those bounds
it held the regulation of opinion to be not only
his right, but his duty, and it did not allow him
arbitrarily to neglect that duty. The tyranny
of the Puritan was thus more equal—more oppres-
sive, for example, in matters of domestic detail;
but his severer laws—*e.g.*, our own statutes against
the idolatry of the mass—were, for some unex-

plained reason—perhaps from some secret instinct
—not carried out; not carried out at least so as
to leave the broadly sanguinary impression which
has stained our historical traditions from the other
side.

In this equipoise the advantage of the popular
party seems to me to have been that they and
their leaders never, at the worst, admitted any
idea of tampering with the sacredness of truth
without and of individual conviction within; that
even when they pressed hardest, in their dogmatic
way, on the individual, they never suggested his
coming over to them except by some process of
reasoned conviction and of private judgment; and
that when they themselves were pressed to conform,
sometimes even by enlightened latitudinarians
like Sir George Mackenzie, with arguments of
torture and death, the flame of loyalty to conscience burned under the pressure only the higher
and the hotter.

And so, with all their short-comings in theory,
they saved the future.

THE QUESTION IN SCOTLAND FIFTY YEARS AGO.

THE QUESTION IN SCOTLAND FIFTY
YEARS AGO.

I.

ONE of my earliest recollections is the rattle of the muskets when a company of soldiers, marched into Easter Ross to keep down the excited population in 1843, grounded their arms in the High Street of the old burgh of Tain. They were drawn up in front of the grey tower on the Castle hill, which half hid the long blue line of Sutherlandshire hills, while far to the right our horizon showed the ruined Keep of Lochslin, the birthplace of the Bloody Mackenzie. It was the centre of a district in which the display of some military force had become necessary. About a year before, the Church of Scotland had solemnly undertaken to disestablish itself; and that promise had now to be fulfilled, but by a very different process from the comfortable euthanasia of retaining a life-interest in the benefices. Most of the

115

Northern ministers adhered to their pledge; but
each of them still held that the church of the
parish belonged to its congregation, and the congregations (who were with them almost unanimously) held still more strongly that the manse
ought to be left with the outgoing minister. That
was not to be. It was found not easy to drive
the Gaelic congregations from the low grey walls
of the Easter Ross churches, each surrounded by
the generations of its dead. And though it was
easy enough to send out from his home each
minister and his family, the actual accomplish-
ment of this, which was now going on, filled every
household in the Highlands with a dangerous mixture of anguish and indignation. In this particular district there were special reasons for
strong feeling. The people were not under the
control of one great proprietor, ducal or otherwise;
but still there were attempts to terrorise. A
powerful landholder in the neighbourhood announced that no labourer should be permitted to
do a stroke of work on his estates, unless on the
previous Sunday he had attended the religious
service provided by the State. The labourers,
backed by their friends in the towns, stood
shoulder to shoulder, and escaped the whole evil
so threatened. But their spiritual leaders, the

ministers in town and country, did not escape from
any part of what had hung over them.

Accordingly, a stranger scene than even that
which Ross-shire peasants and burghers now gazed
upon had been transacted a few days before in
the metropolis of Scotland. It was a grey and
cloudy afternoon on the ridge of the new town
of Edinburgh, where masses of spectators gathered
in breathless expectation round the tall spire of
St. Andrew's Church. Into its interior, crowded
since early dawn with a like eager multitude, the
members of Assembly and the glittering *cortége*
of the Queen's Commissioner had just disappeared.
The doors were now shut, and all Scotland seemed
to wait outside. Suddenly they were broken
open, and a roar of acclamation rent the air as
the ex-Moderator in his robes, and by his side the
venerable face of Chalmers, were seen to appear.
For following these two came the leaders of the
Evangelical revival in the Church of Scotland from
Highlands and Lowlands alike. The crowd surged
in emotion around them, so as to make the old
men in front the head of an involuntary procession.
It took a few steps westward, and then, turning
to the right, moved down the steep brow of that
long slope which connects northern Edinburgh
with the sea. One by one the ministers then in

Edinburgh, who had resolved to cast in their lot
with the Church, fell into the moving line. But
after them marched a train of young men, " licen-
tiates " or candidates, who had looked forward to
its benefices, but who (like all its missionaries
without exception in foreign lands) chose now to
belong to this its forlorn hope. Together they
set their faces to the long descent into that valley
of humiliation. Before them the waters of the
Firth gleamed under the blue and bitter north,
and beyond it stretched many a moor and strath,
with the manses which the old men were in a few
weeks to leave and the young men were never to
enter.

To one of those manses I had paid an unseason-
able morning visit two months before. There was
a bright March sunrise, and I had jumped early
out of bed, for my head was full of marbles and
peg-tops, and a dozen or so of games before break-
fast has, at that age, its attractions. To my
astonishment, I found my father down before me ;
indeed, he had evidently been there for some time,
for the moment I appeared he folded up the newspaper in which he had been so unseasonably
engaged, and—with a break in his voice indicating
an emotion that was unaccountable to me—asked
me to take it at once over to the manse, with his

compliments to his friend the minister. I went very readily, for the hedgerows were full of young birds upon whom legitimate hostilities could be waged in passing. But as I went I reflected on the austere and stately image of our pastor,— a man everywhere venerated, but whose face inspired awe rather than love in the beholder—(had I not seen the town-boys break and scatter round one corner of the street as he appeared at the other?)—and I resolved that my interview with him should be short. It was shorter than I expected, for I had scarcely got out of the sunshine into the manse evergreens, when I found him in the porch; and when I offered him the newspaper, he showed me that he had already got the *Times* by some unusual express, and as he spoke he patted my head and smiled—but such a smile, so full of radiant kindliness! I was confounded; and as I went back between the hedges the birds sang unheeded while I thought what could have happened to the minister. Had anybody left him a fortune? or had he met one of the Shining Ones walking among the hollies in that early dawn? And it was not for some weeks that I found out that this was what had happened—the newspaper that morning had brought him the vote of the House of Commons, finally refusing an inquiry into the affairs of the Scottish Church, and so making it certain that within a few weeks he and his aged mother would leave for ever the home, at the door of which I found him.

But the "gentleness and gaiety" of heart with which we are told, in a memorable passage of Lord Cockburn,[1] that the country ministers faced the coming of the crisis, did not free them from having to go through with it afterwards in all its grinding detail. This was the point of one of the most striking reminiscences of Dr. Thomas Guthrie at a later date. " I remember passing a manse on a moonlight night, with the minister who had left it, for the cause of truth. No light shone from the house, and no smoke arose. Pointing to it in the moonlight, I said, 'Oh, my friend, it was a noble thing to leave that house.' 'Ah, yes,' he replied; 'it was a noble thing, but for all that it was a bitter thing. I shall never forget the night I left that house till I am laid in my grave. When I saw my wife and children go forth in the gloaming; when I saw them for the last time leave our own door; and when in the dark I was left alone, with none but my God in that house; and when I had to take water and quench the fire on my own hearth, and put out the candle in my

---

[1] *Journal of Henry Cockburn*, II., 32.

own house, and turn the key against myself, and
my wife, and my little ones that night—God in His
mercy grant that such a night I may never again
see !'" Those who left their homes at once, as
most in Ross-shire were now doing, had perhaps the
best of it. But some were gladly allowed to linger
on till the early Northern winter. "One minister
writes to us that he left the manse with his family
in a snow storm, when the mountain was white
with snow, and the sky was black with drift; but
that he never knew so much of the peace of God
as he did that night, when following his wife and
children as they were carted over the mountain,
without knowing where they were to find a place
to dwell in. Some of our ministers write that
they live in crofters' houses; some in places as
damp as cellars, where a candle will not burn.
One says he sits with his great coat on; another
that the curtains of his bed shake at night like
the sails of a ship in a storm. One minister, a
friend of mine, lives in a house which every wind
of heaven blows through. On getting up one
morning he found the house all comparatively
comfortable, and wondered what good genius had
been putting it in order, when he discovered that
a heavy shower of snow had fallen, and stopped
up the crevices of the roof."

It must always be remembered that the country,
and especially the Highlands, were different in this
respect from the great towns, even after that first
winter of 1843.   It was some years before the
Northern manses were built, and homelessness,
added to poverty, pressed heavily on the ejected
ministers.   I remember how, as a boy, I used to
watch one of them, a scholarly, and in his college
days a rather distinguished man, who after 1843
was unable to find a home within his own parish,
and who besides now laboured under a weak chest
and a threatening of heart complaint.   Yet week
after week, as each Sunday morning came round,
he persisted in driving away for miles through
those inclement winters to meet his congregation ;
and I can remember to this day his keen, delicate
face set to meet a heavy snow-storm from the north-
west, while a hacking cough shook his whole frame
as he set out on his journey, four miles of which
must pass ere he caught sight of the well-sheltered
and well-remembered manse.   But those who, like
him, found shelter in a town dwelling, however
humble, were not worst off.   The great difficulty
was in the country, even when harbouring the
minister was not forbidden by the great landlords.
But in many cases, and occasionally over whole
districts or counties, it was forbidden.   And where

a foot of ground was forbidden to the minister,
as well as to his congregation, the results, always
depressing to him, and cruelly distressing to his
family, sometimes reached a pitch of strange and
memorable oppression. I have myself often con-
versed with the minister of "Small Isles"—four
inhabited rocks clustering together out in the
wild Atlantic—whose ministry, forbidden on those
morsels of the land, was carried on in the boat
upon the billow which his school friend, Hugh
Miller, celebrated as the Floating Manse. And
I stood as a boy in the mighty cavern near Cape
Wrath beside the pure-hearted pastor who, when
ejected with his people from their church and
manse on the ground of a site-refusing Duke,[1]
worshipped throughout the winter under those
humid arches, while the only "life interests" conceded him were in the savage rock and resounding
shore.

In the awakening of thought which such scenes
stirred in the young, there was a strong moral
element, not stimulating only, but animating.
"All good things have not kept aloof, nor wandered into other ways," was the irrepressible

[1] Not the Duke who may be remembered by readers of
Carlyle as the opponent of Janet Fraser. See Froude's
Life of Carlyle, III., 322.

feeling of lads who had been drifting on towards
the dull afternoon of the century, and were suddenly surrounded by this illuminating glow. Apparently then, their country, too, was to have
a future as well as a past. For it was plain,
even in 1843, that the great event of that year
was essentially transitional. It left Scotland in
a state of unstable equilibrium, and confronted
it with a problem, political no doubt, but moral
as well. And what might a history not call for
in the future which revealed such gulfs and
altitudes in the present? What might such a
country not yet claim of its sons? Above all,
what did it not already deserve at their hands?
Those of them who are most conscious of having
failed in obedience to the early vision, do yet,
in looking back, recognise the nobility of its call
—a call which they have found most noble and
most adequate precisely when they are brought
nearest to some crisis of public duty. Those, on
the other hand, who "think they pay every debt
to virtue when they praise it," have never had
a comfortable time in Scotland. The occasions
for not merely admiring but imitating return too
frequently. And for some time past there has
been a well-founded apprehension in all parts of
the Scottish Church that its complete freedom

or its complete union may involve some of its members in a share—say, one-sixteenth or one-sixtieth part—of the same self-sacrifice as was shown in 1843.   That, of course, is not a plea that can be nakedly stated, nor is it one which many men in their hearts entertain.   The mass of the Scottish people, even when within the establishment, hold the principles which in that year drove their brethren out of it.   And the only recent occasions, when illusory legislation in its favour has had even a passing chance of success, were when it was promised as "on the lines of 1843," or as "all that was asked for" in that year. But the contact of the unsatisfied claim of past history with the demand of present duty is far too suggestive to be safe; and from time to time we hear, even in Scotland, unmeaning and gratuitous protests that the Disruption happened a long time ago—that it is now happily forgotten—and that, perhaps, to tell the truth, it never deserved to be remembered.   As Free Churchmen born in the Scottish Highlands hear these recurrent clamours, we seem to see rising before us once more those grave suffering faces, most of them by this time gone down into a deeper silence; and the utterance of their stillness is not unlike that of our new Norse poet,—

" When thou hearest the fool rejoicing, and he saith, ' It
    is over and past,
And the wrong was better than right, and hate turns into
    love at the last ;
And we strove for nothing at all, and the gods have fallen
    asleep,
For so good the world is growing that the evil good shall
    reap,'
Then loosen thy sword in the scabbard, and settle the helm
    on thy head,
For men betrayed are mighty, and great are the wrongfully
    dead."

But may the dead not have made a heroic
mistake ? Was there, after all, any reason why
they should sacrifice themselves and go out ? The
answer must be given ; but readers who find constitutional facts too dry may pass over the next
few pages.

II.

In Scotland, which, as a whole, has been Presbyterian since the Reformation, the Church party
has generally been the popular party. What is
more strange to English ears, the Evangelical
party has, on the whole, been the Church party,
all revival here of religious feeling or individual
conviction tending to take shape in public and
organised action. Ten years before 1843 the
General Assembly, or representative body of the

ministers and laity of the Church, had begun to
show an "evangelical majority." It at once set
about the work of Church reform, and especially
of Church expansion, in two directions. The
Church, by its own authority, welcomed to a seat
in its courts the pastors of the two hundred new
congregations, which had been gathered together
chiefly through the devotion and eloquence of Dr.
Chalmers. At the same time, and in the same
way, it admitted a considerable number of Original
Secession and other ministers who had returned
to the reviving Establishment. Church Extension
and Church Union, indeed, were supposed to be
the great aggressive duties of the new time ; and
the fact that ordinary Church administration has
always been left in Scotland to the Church itself—
the ordinary jurisdiction of its courts has never
been interfered with either before or after 1843—
naturally led to the belief that Church legislation
and Church development might also be free. This
was found to be a mistake, and the refusal of
places and votes to those who had been admitted
by the Ecclesiastical body was in the long run the
immediate cause of the Protest and Disruption
of 1843. But the third and earliest occasion of
the quarrel with the State was the old question
of patronage, which has broken out in so many

lands, and which, under the name of Investiture, caused, in the eleventh century, the greatest conflict of Church and State which the world has seen. In Scotland, however, the veto upon arbitrary nomination by a patron was now declared to belong, not to pope, churchman, or chapter, but to the whole "congregation of the faithful people." And this third measure was represented by the Assembly which passed it in 1834, as a defensive rather than aggressive regulation—founded, indeed, on what was at all times a "fundamental law of the Church." Suddenly, in the midst of so much expansive energy and enthusiasm, a crushing blow fell upon them. All three reforms were declared by the Law Courts to be incompetent; but what was far more alarming was the ground on which in each case the conclusion was based. It was, that the Scottish Establishment is absolutely subject, even in matters ecclesiastical, to the State and to its enactments, past and future.

The present constitutional law, that the Church of Scotland is *in no sense independent of the State, but is absolutely subject to Parliament and to Statute,* was then, for the first time, solemnly laid down. Take the three heads of the Court alone. President Hope put it thus: " That our Saviour is the Head of the Kirk of Scotland in any temporal, or legislative, or judicial sense, is a position which I can signify by no other name than absurdity. The Parliament is the temporal head of the Church, from whose acts, and from whose acts alone, it exists as the National Church, and from which alone it derives all its powers." Again, "Who gave the Church courts any jurisdiction? The law and that alone *gave* it; and the law defines what it has so given." And as the Church was not independent, they denied the possibility of any original compact, or of any real conflict, between Church and State, as an "indecent supposition." Even the courts of the State were entitled to fix for the Church its separate province granted by the State. So President Boyle : "There exists, in reality, no such thing as a conflict between the civil and ecclesiastical courts of a country, in which a church is established and endowed by the State." And so Lord Justice-Clerk Hope : "I cannot admit that an Establishment can ever possess an independent jurisdiction."

And of course, on these principles, the courts made short work of the claim, that the Church was not bound to obey Acts of Parliament which proposed to regulate spiritual or Church actings. Several of the judges put it that the Church is " the creature of Statute ;" all of them that it is bound

9

to obey Statutes which regulate, or, in its own
view, interfere with, its proper church action.
Take again only two of the utterances, and both
from the chair of the court.   In the third Auchterarder case, the Presbytery had pleaded that
what they were called on to do was strictly
ecclesiastical, was against their conscience, and
against the commands of the Church.   Lord Justice-Clerk Hope answered that although these
functions are "strictly ecclesiastical, and to be
exercised by them in their ecclesiastical capacity,
yet the obligation to perform them is statutory—
Statute imposes the duty on the Church courts of
the establishment," and the courts must enforce
the statute.   And when in the still higher sphere
of the House of Lords it had been pleaded in addition, that there was a "fundamental law" of the
Church of Scotland which forbade such Church
action, even in compliance with statute, the Lord
Chancellor of Great Britain, sitting as chief of
the Jurisprudence of Scotland, enounced the
general rule which has ever since been the law,
as follows : "Whether that is, or ever was, a law
of the Church of Scotland, is *perfectly immaterial*,
if the Statutes contain enactments and confer
rights inconsistent with any such principle, or
with the execution of any such law."   It followed

that the Church and its office-bearers were bound
legally, and if they accepted the law would be
bound legally and morally, to obey any statute
the State might pass in the future, no matter how
inconsistent it might be with the present or past
principles of the Church—to obey it not merely
passively, but actively, and as ecclesiastical functionaries. The obligation of individuals to obey
actively received great prominence at an early
stage of the decisions; but before their close it
was plain that on the principles now laid down
the Church itself was in a worse case. For, in
the event of its being thereafter dissatisfied with
these or any worse incidents of its connection
with the State, it would have no power either to
abandon that connection, or to treat for new terms
as a party able to accept or to refuse.

This is the present law of establishment in
Scotland, unchanged since 1843 ; and the principles
I have quoted ·were laid down in great leading
cases with cumulative emphasis and solemnity.[1]
But all of them were in themselves general statements of law, addressed to the constitutional
question of Church independence,—a question
which did not depend on the special matters of

[1] See for details a pamphlet of 1875 entitled, The Scotch
Law of Establishment.

non-intrusion or Church extension, though they depended upon it. They were given as the ground, and they were the ground, of the innumerable decisions and orders of the court enforced against the Church. And they were intended to settle, and they did settle, what both parties knew and confessed to be the great constitutional question then in dependence.

How opposed they are to the ancient theory held by the Church as to its independence I need not here say. But the law laid down long before May 1843 would have abundantly justified it even then in separating from the State, protesting that its constitutional liberties had been authoritatively subverted. Fortunately for the future of the country, it did otherwise. It appealed to the State itself, that is, to the Legislature and the Crown, against the decision of the judicial organs of the State. And it was only upon their neglect— and indeed rejection—of the Claim, Declaration, and Protest of 1842, that the Free Church went out in 1843. But when it did so, it combined the two considerations, of the authority of the Courts on the constitutional question, and the supereminent power of the Legislature, with great felicity, in its Protest, which ran :—

" Considering that the Legislature, by their

rejection, etc., . . . have recognised and fixed the
conditions of the Church Establishment, as henceforward to subsist in Scotland, *to be such as these
have been pronounced and declared* by the said Civil
Courts, in their several recent decisions, in regard
to matters spiritual and ecclesiastical."

The one matter on which the Civil and Church
Courts, otherwise so keenly opposed, were agreed,
was this, that the claim of the Church was really
one of independence—independence not merely of
the Civil Courts, but of the State and Parliament.
Therefore it became necessary for the Civil Courts,
in enforcing their decrees against it, in matters
ecclesiastical, to affirm its dependence upon both
in the broad terms we have quoted.   And therefore also the Church, in taking up its position in
the Act of Assembly 1838, affirming " the independent jurisdiction," put it upon the ground that
the " power ecclesiastical flows immediately from
God " to the Church, and not through the mediation
of the State or Parliament.   But what probability
was there that the Scottish Church could persuade
the Legislature of Great Britain in 1842, to affirm
such an abstract proposition as this in regard to
one of its Established Churches ?   None whatever.   Its only chance was that the Legislature
might so far interfere as to prevent the *enforce-*

ment of the orders and interdicts already based by the Court upon these general principles. In that case the Church could perhaps have honestly stayed in, as standing upon its own declaration of independence; the denial of which by the Courts they would then have regarded as *brutum fulmen*, and no longer authoritative, because, at least virtually, disclaimed by the State. Even early in 1842 both parties were thus already agreed that the practical question must decide the constitutional question. Was the Church to obey, or was it not ?[1]

The Church made the most of its last hope in that massive and magnificent state-paper, the Claim, Declaration, and Protest of 1842; in which, while founding its jurisdiction not on law but on Gospel, and protesting that it was for maintaining the Headship of Christ and not of

---

[1] The result of compliance, first to the Church and then to its individual members, was thus put: "They surely do not remember what, in her case, their judgment implies, who say that until the Law of Patronage should be altered by the Legislature, and placed by that authority in a position more consonant with the constitutional principles to which she appeals against it, the Ecclesiastical tribunals of the Church ought to have given implicit obedience to those legal decisions which proceeded upon its yet unmodified provisions. . . . They forget that as an embody-

the State over the Church that it was called to
suffer, it laid at the same time great stress on the
limited and civil jurisdiction of the Court of Session. And while it enumerated here, as afterwards
in its separating Protest, the long roll of cases in
which the Court enforced the State's supremacy
even *in spiritualibus,*—by which, "no one function
of the Church," "and no one item mentioned by
the laws as belonging peculiarly to its judgment,"
had been spared,—it passed over in silence the loud
denials of Church independence upon which these
encroachments were based. But what it did not
omit was to affirm its own independence, and
solemnly to "declare" to both Houses of Parliament and the Crown, that the Church could not
in conscience obey or submit as the Court
demanded, and that "at the risk of losing the
public advantages of an Establishment" they

---

ing and representation of certain principles of faith and
discipline, she loses her identity when she ceases to hold
to these. They forget that ministers and office-bearers,
whose strict adherence to the fundamental principles upon
which the institutes of their Church are founded, forms
their only right to the station they occupy, can never feel
themselves at liberty to compromise their integrity by acts
for which they are individually responsible."—*Letter to
the Peers* in 1842 by Lord Lorne (the present Duke of
Argyll).

" must, as by God's grace they will, refuse to do
so ; for, highly as they estimate these, they cannot
put them in competition with the inalienable
liberties of a Church of Christ." The claim was
rejected by the other great parties concerned with
an equally fatal explicitness. Crown and Legislature declined to interfere ; and that not merely
tacitly, which would have been abundantly enough.
In the answer from the advisers of the Crown,[1]
and in the refusal of the House of Commons[2] to
entertain even a motion for enquiry, it was no
doubt not concealed that they were zealous for the
existence of Patronage, and knew the Church to
be pledged against it. But in both of them the
refusal was put explicitly upon the constitutional
question stated by the Court, by the Assembly,
and in the Claim of Rights, as the only one of chief
importance ; and the legislative interference which
all parties looked forward to was delayed in order,
as the Prime Minister put it expressly in the
House, that the pretensions of the Church to
independence and co-ordinate jurisdiction might
be *first* surrendered or crushed. I know not how
a constitutional question such as the future rela-

---

[1] Letter of Sir James Graham, 4th January, 1843.
[2] 7th and 8th March, 1843.

tion of Church and State could be more solemnly
and conclusively settled, than (first) by the
authoritative and repeated utterances of the
Supreme Courts, appealed against (secondly) by
the National Church as fatal to its very existence,
and (lastly) confirmed upon this appeal by the
supreme power of the State as before all things
necessary and right.

And yet this was not all—not nearly all.   It
might have been a mere abstract question that
was thus solemnly settled.   But this abstract
question was to be settled, as we have seen, by
the practical method of enforced obedience, and
the *constitutional disturbance* attending it amounted
to a long agony.   Even before 1842 the Church
and its Courts had solemnly protested that it
could not obey the State *in spiritualibus* in the
matters already enjoined it.   And so during the
eighteen months that followed, while it made its
vain appeal to the Legislature, the mace of the
law fell heavily and cruelly upon every part of
the ecclesiastical body.   In Perthshire, in Ayrshire, in Aberdeenshire, in every corner of the
country, the principle of subjection to a civil
statute in ecclesiastical matters was enforced by
fines and interdicts, until the Church at last went
out bruised in every quivering limb.   But these

sufferings—and even the fines and expenses which
some of the houseless ministers had to pay, after
being turned out of their livings—were not felt
so much by the Church as the taunts which
accompanied them.   The Court of Session, in
utterance as well as action, refused to tolerate
even that *interim* refusal to obey ,while the
Church was making its appeal to the Legislature.
" I wish," said Lord President Hope, speaking as
the head of the Court,[1] " to speak with all respect
of the General Assembly, of which body I was for
so long a period a member; but if any other body
of men, or if any individuals had done what they
have done, I should feel constrained to designate
their conduct as profligate.   The Presbytery of
Auchterarder came to this Court and pleaded
here. Judgment went against them.   The General
Assembly sanctioned and directed an appeal to
the House of Lords. . . . But the decision of the
House of Lords affirmed the decision of this Court,
and these same Church Courts absolutely refuse
to give obedience to the judgment.   To conduct
like this I have already given its appropriate
designation.   In point of candour and fairness it
is no better than the old shuffle, 'Odds I win,

----

[1] The quotations are from Dunlop's *Reports.*

evens you lose.'" And this terrible imputation of
dishonesty, flung from the judgment-seat against
those who should continue to eat the bread of the
State, and yet refuse the legal conditions of establishment, was repeated more decorously again
and again as the case went on. "If these gentlemen," said President Hope in the second Auchterarder Case, "wish to maintain the situation of
what they call a Christian Church, they would be
no better off than the Catholic Church, or the
Episcopal Church, or the Burghers or Anti-
Burghers; but when they come to call themselves
the Established Church, the Church of Scotland,
what makes the Church of Scotland but the
Law?" And the House of Lords was equally
intolerant of men claiming to be free who remained in this law-made Church. "It is fit,"
said Lord Brougham in the same case in the
House of Lords, "that these men at length learn
the lesson of obedience to the tribunals which
have been appointed over them; a lesson which
all others have long acquired, and which they,
on learning it, should also practise." And this
obedience, Lord Campbell went on immediately to
explain, could not be evaded by those "who continue members of the Establishment" abandoning
the temporalities to the State or the patron.

Disestablishment was the only honest remedy.
"While the appellants remain members of the
establishment, they are, in addition to their
sacred character, public functionaries appointed
and paid by the State, and they must perform
the duties which the law of the land imposes on
them. It is only a voluntary body, such as the
Relief or Burgher Church in Scotland, self-founded
and self-supported, that can say they will be
entirely governed by their own rules." Now all
these, whether we call them kindly suggestions
or cruel taunts or statements of principle, came
from the Supreme Courts as parts of their solemn
judgments, and were authoritative. We need not
therefore recall the far more violent attacks on
the Church in the Legislature, the demand of the
Moderate[1] League, that the Government should
choose which of the two parties was to remain in
the Establishment, and the bitter inculpation
of the Whig government by the Conservatives
generally, and Lords Aberdeen and Brougham in
particular, for its hesitation to enforce the new

---

[1] "Throughout this Letter I shall use this term to
designate all those who now oppose the Church's views,
and unite in the accusations of disobedience. It has
every recommendation, *except that of being descriptive.*"
—Lord Lorne's *Letter to the Peers.*

constitutional law. For the great strength of these hostile utterances during that last lingering year of the controversy, was that *they were true*— that the Church knew them to be true, and had made them part of its principles. The right of the State to fix its own conditions of establishment, whether those conditions be right or wrong, had been admitted in the most absolute way in the Church's Claim, Declaration, and Protest of 1842, and is made the foundation of the Free Church Protest in 1843. We, looking back, may be disposed to think that the denial of Church independence and the demand of subjection to Statute, affirmed by the Courts in and before 1842, were final conditions of Establishment even then, and that they might have come out before. But it is not for us harshly to judge Churchmen, who at the cost of uninterrupted taunts and insults, clung to the State till every method of appeal was exhausted—till, in fact (as comes out so curiously in the Protest of 1843), waiting in for a *quarter of an hour* longer had become practically and morally impossible. For thus it was that the constitutional question of subjection, now broadly separated from the previous one of patronage, and already decided by the Supreme Courts, was with due solemnity

referred by the National Church to the Crown
and Legislature, and was deliberately decided by
the Legislature and the Crown.

There are countries in which even this accumulation of reasons would not amount to reason
for revolution; for in these lands the original
independence of the Christian Church has faded
out of the convictions of men. But in a country
with such a history as Scotland, the Disruption
was a necessity of conscience. It was not the
less a memorable self-sacrifice. A quarter of an
hour after it happened the news was brought to
Lord Jeffrey as he sat in his room, and the old
judge, springing from his seat, exclaimed, " I am
proud of my country; there is not another upon
earth where such a deed could have been done ! "
A quarter of a century after it happened Mr.
Gladstone, speaking as Prime Minister in his
place in Parliament, proclaimed that to the moral
attitude of the new-born Church " scarcely any
word weaker or lower than that of majesty, is,
according to the spirit of historical criticism, justly
applicable." But the more that Scotland recog-
nises the deed of 1843 as flowing from her previous
history and ancient convictions, the less will she
be disposed to dwell upon it in any mood of
transient exultation. Rather she will hear its

voice at the close of the half-century as the same great Saga[1] speaks it,—

" Wilt thou do the deed and repent it? Thou had'st better never been born.
Wilt thou do the deed and exalt it? Then thy praise shall be outworn.
Thou shalt *do the deed and abide it*, and sit on thy throne on high,
And look on to-day and to-morrow as those that never die!"

III.

But, in truth, the deed of 18th May, 1843, is one which will never need to be repeated. What must in some form be repeated, and what may in many forms require to be imitated or improved upon—what, therefore, now deserves study not from Churchmen or Scotsmen alone—is the re-construction by which that deed was followed. For the reconstruction was the act of the people. " Contrary to all anticipations, the people had forsaken the establishment in a much higher ratio as to numbers than the ministers; and it would have required more than seven hundred churches to accommodate the congregations who were ready to attach themselves to the Free Church." Around us in the Highlands this side of the thing

[1] William Morris' *Sigurd the Volsung.*

came out very strongly. Where the minister had
resigned his living, the people followed him enthusiastically; where he did not, they left him in a
body. But in the Highlands, as much as in the
Lowlands, an almost hopeless problem remained.
In some places the people were numerous, but they
were poor. In others they were a little better off,
but they were few. But neither in the Highlands
nor in the Lowlands had they been trained to act
for themselves. It was a feudal country, and the
natural leaders of the people—the chiefs in the
north, like the lairds in the south—had in this
matter failed them. Local self-government was
not yet thought of. Voluntary parochial union
had been evoked by Dr. Chalmers, and was one
of the things now being crushed. But mere
parochial union could not solve the problem how
things were to be carried on upon a national scale,
and for all time to come. In previous national
efforts Scotsmen had the civil law of the nation
behind them, obliging all citizens to religious
union, and appropriating to the uses of the
majority, in the name of their common country,
the fruits and possessions of those who should
refuse to obey. In the present case that law was
no longer at their back; in so far as it survived,
it worked now to enfeeble and impoverish them.

The experiment, whether a whole people could be banded together to work out by means of individual self-sacrifice one great common and permanent result, was to be tried under new conditions. And some of the conditions were not only new, but hard.

For all over Scotland the congregations called to this problem were left houseless in one day. In one class of cases alone they earnestly attempted to save themselves. The Church Extension edifices had been raised chiefly, in some cases almost wholly, by the money of those who were now members of the Free Church, and the ministers officiating in them had been denied recognition by the Courts on the ground that they and their congregations were wholly a creation of the Church. But even these churches were now taken by the Courts from the Church which had erected them, and that on the paradoxical ground that they had been erected for the Church of the State. In south and north alike the congregations had thus to seek immediate shelter from the elements, as well as sites for more permanent homes of worship. But in south and north even sites for building were very often denied them. And this brought up, for the second time in this century,

that inevitable Land Question which, in the
previous generation, had been stirred in our
Highlands by the bitterly remembered "clearances." The amazing power which our law
entrusts to private landholders, of excluding a
whole community from purchasing a foot of
ground in their own parish, or even their own
county, came out now for the first time in its
intolerable extent. The clearances had sometimes
swept out whole bodies or communities. "I stood
on the top of that hill when the evictions were
going on," an old Sutherlandshire woman said to
me, speaking of her youthful days, "and I saw
sixty cottages burning in the strath at one time."
And I well remember the consternation in the
Gaelic congregation to which in her age she
belonged, when, one morning after 1843, the
announcement of an interdict drove them out
from an ancient churchyard—a churchyard, too,
distant half a mile from the parish church—
amid whose moss-grown stones the people had met
for many and many a sacrament before that
mournful day. The preacher, who was that
Sabbath to address four or five thousand Gaelic
hearers, was Dr. John Macdonald of Ferintosh;
and he pointed out, whether by way of defence or of aggravation, that the ground from

which the people of the parish were so driven out
was common and parochial property. The more
usual case was that which happened, at almost
the same time, to Dr. Thomas Guthrie of Edinburgh. In this case the Duke—Janet Fraser's
Duke—was proprietor of the parish, and as land-
lord refused a site. The miserable people quietly
withdrew to a waste spot of barren moor, and met
there in the open air. The Duke's factor and
agent instantly served an interdict on the tres-
passers, evicting them from even their open-air
meeting on the waste. Henceforth they had no
place on which to worship except the cross-roads
on the public highway, and one Monday morning,
after preaching to them there, Dr. Guthrie sat
down to tell his experiences. " Well wrapped up,
I drove out yesterday morning to Canobie, the
hills white with snow, the roads covered ankle-
deep in many places with slush, the wind high
and cold, thick rain lashing on, and the Esk by
our side all the way, roaring in the snowflood
between bank and brae. We passed Johnnie
Armstrong's Tower, yet strong even in its ruins,
and after a drive of four miles, a turn of the road
brought me in view of a scene which was overpowering, and would have brought the salt tears
into the eyes of any man of common humanity."

Dr. Guthrie's driver broke into sobs as he explained that the five hundred people waiting under some leafless trees on the turnpike road were the congregation who had been refused first a site to build, and then a site to stand upon; and who now waited on for hours under the driving rain till they had sung their last psalm on that fierce February day. It was not there only. So late as 1847 there were still thirty-one cases in Scotland in which sites were absolutely refused; besides many others in which very inconvenient and humiliating places were deliberately offered—offered, too, to tenants who frequently had the threat of eviction held over them if they ventured to build even upon these.

Now what was the problem which the laymen of this Scottish Church, itself universally left houseless, had first of all to face? It was not their own support, but that of their ministers and of many besides. The income of every Free Church minister ceased at Whitsunday, 1843, and at the same date ceased his tenancy of the "manse" or parsonage, with its "glebe" of four acres of parochial ground. But along with them one hundred and thirty "probationers," or preachers waiting for appointments, had, on the same day, thrown up all their prospects. The foreign missionaries sent out to India, with Dr. Duff at their head, had likewise, without exception, sent in their adherence to the disendowed community. An old statute obliged all teachers, within or without the Universities, to be members of the Establishment, and the theological professors who, like Dr. Chalmers, had moved with the Church, were by this enactment obliged to resign their posts. A more cruel case remained. Every parish schoolmaster throughout Scotland who adhered to the Church going out was ejected from his small house, and deprived of his income. Ministers, missionaries, probationers, schoolmasters, and professors were in a day reduced to beggary. A small army of educated men, with their families, were left destitute and houseless, and thrown upon the congregations whose own necessities we have seen. In the days to come many hard questions will have to be dealt with in our own and other lands. The rights of labour, the claims of the poor, the division of the soil, the education of the young, the home-rule of our young empires, and the self-support of the Church—all these will bring round many a crisis in many a family of Western man. But can any of them ever present a harder problem than our fathers in Scotland had that day to solve?

Yet it was done—by Christian enthusiasm, no
doubt. But that enthusiasm found or made fit
channels for its flow. And among these we may
mention first what is familiar in Scotland, but
most strikes the observer outside. "The Kirk," Sir
Roundell Palmer told the House of Commons in
1869, "had her Kirk Sessions, her Presbyteries,
her Synods, her General Assemblies, each step of
self-government rising above the other, so that she
had been well exercised in the whole art and power
of self-government, self-legislation, and self-expansion, no State power coming in to prevent her
Synods from meeting. There the great men who
afterwards became the leaders in the Free Church
movement had as much liberty of speech as we
have in this place. There they formed their
parties; there they organised their system; there
they collected together such a power and bond of
moral public opinion as enabled them to go forth
triumphantly, even when leaving all which in this
world they possessed." It is a lesson for us all.
For in Scotland, as elsewhere, there are now men
who hate the whole system of Parliamentarism,
in Church and State alike; men who would rather
shelter under any form of epicurean despotism
than take their share of the risks and responsibilities of self-government. But that system has

great tasks still to accomplish in the future, and there is no surer omen of its victory in these than that under it, in 1843, the terrible crisis of Disestablishment was carried through. It was carried through, indeed, with scarcely any constitutional change. The Church remained the same, except as now founded on its Protest for freedom. The Presbyteries which had sat the week before as Courts of the Church of Scotland established, sat this week again—with frightful gaps and rents no doubt—but as Courts of the same Church unestablished. Legislation was held now, as before, to belong to its General Assembly, with consent of the Presbyteries; for the refusal of the State to permit this, the Church had met by the last remedy. And none of these Church Courts are mere " convocations of the clergy;" in all of them the representative layman, elected by the whole members of the congregation, decides upon the most sacred matters, with a vote equal to that of the Churchman at his side. And as with " self-government " and " self-legislation," so with the third function assigned to our classic hierarchy by Lord Selborne—" self-expansion." Its rights of creating new congregations, recognising new ministers, and incorporating with itself other religious bodies—all repressed with fines and pro-

hibitions only a few months before—were now
exercised freely. It was all within the common
law of Presbyterianism—a code of authoritative
principles, whose breadth, forgotten so long as our
branch of the system flowed in a merely national
and statutory channel, was soon to be restored to
the view of all in the ecumenical assemblies or
Councils of the communion.

But the feature in the new organisation of
most interest, not so much in the past as for the
future of our own and other lands, was what Dr.
Chalmers, with his usual passion for sonorous
phraseology, called a Sustentation Fund.[1] It was,
in truth, a new and great experiment in altruism
or Christian solidarity. The local enthusiasm
which had everywhere arisen of course received
fit embodiment. Long before the Disruption Dr.
Chalmers had given forth as his watchword,
"Organise, organise, organise!" And while in response congregational associations were everywhere
instituted, and great numbers of women collectors
gathered weekly the contributions of the faithful,
the old order of deacons was revived for what was
supposed to have been in apostolic times their
exclusive function—the receiving and administer-

[1] The name, and within municipal limits the thing, go
back to John Knox.

ing of the monies of the local church. But through all these organisations there passed the breath of one new life, when, in autumn 1842, it was proposed that they should no longer retain their own contributions for their separate benefit, but should send the mass of them on to one central fund for the Church as a whole, to be again divided equally from that centre among all the ministers. The idea was almost new then, but in that time · of common suffering it commended itself irresistibly; and it has ever since been acted on to an extraordinary extent. Some Free Church congregations send to the Sustentation Fund annually from £1,000 to £3,000; others in poorer districts can only send from £10 to £50. But the small and the large contribution go alike into the common purse, and, as the time of annual division comes round, the minister of the poorer congregation receives from it the same amount as the minister of the greater—no less, and no more. This national voluntaryism, as Dr. Chalmers pointed out, really becomes an establishment of the Church from its own resources, and while it " coincides in principle " with that former method of support, it is free from some of its obvious disadvantages. In particular, it leaves to the Church itself the more complicated adjustment of

the remaining question, how the salary from this
equal dividend may be locally added to. For,
as Dr. Chalmers originally urged, mere equality
would not be justice where one minister with
city burdens was giving up a stipend of £1,000
a year, and another in the country lost only £200.
Besides, it is not even desirable that the minister
of a congregation, however he may be protected
by the Central Fund from the possibility of being
starved out, should be removed from the stimulus
which most other workers have in the prospect
of a larger income for successful work. How all
this was met by the institution of congregational
supplements,—a variable accretion of local voluntaryism, added on to the solid nucleus of the
Church's own establishment in the Sustentation Fund;—and how the two combined have,
through many years of not yet ended experiment,
become a backbone to the Free Church (a backbone whose value seems to be owing nearly
equally to its firmness and its flexibility), we need
not here inquire.[1]   What is important to notice

---

[1] An account of the institution of the whole finance of
the Free Church, including that of the Sustentation Fund,
and of the first twenty-five years of its development, will
be found (drawn from the annual official documents) in
the *British Quarterly* for January 1870.

is, that the idea which it embodies, which men
have now come to speak of as a kind of national
altruism, pressed outwards at the same time in
many other directions, and beyond all merely
patriotic bounds. We have seen the houseless-
ness of the congregations in every county throughout the hard north. But a hundred thousand
pounds were subscribed for building even before
the Disruption day dawned, and within the first
year five hundred churches were erected. Then
came the effort necessary to provide manses
or pastorages for the ministers. And then it
was recollected that the evicted schoolmasters
and their children were homeless too. Yet all
this concerned no city Scotsman who doubted
whether he were his brother's keeper, and who
reflected that the raising of such edifices implied
a certain obligation in all time coming to
those for whom they were built. Almost the
only enterprise indeed, in which the centres
were not able to sacrifice themselves for those
outside, was the raising of the three colleges—two
of them soon permanently endowed by private
munificence, and the third now, with all its imperfections, the most fully equipped theological
institute in theological Scotland. But the impulse was one which, in its own nature, could not

be restricted to self-regarding or self-conserving
effort. All the missionaries had joined the Church
in its conflict, and, as might be expected, all
now fulfilled their pledge. But the disestablished
Church, instead of recalling them, commenced to
double, and more than double, the sum previously
sent out to maintain them. Missions to spread
Christianity among the Jews followed, and missions to fan the flame of evangelism in Catholic
countries. New missions to colonies, where Scotsmen so abound, could scarcely be called outside
enterprises ; and these bring us back to the special
funds instituted for the Highlands and Islands, and
to the new and great enterprise of a Home Mission,
partly consisting of Extension Charges throughout
the country, and partly of Territorial Charges,
"excavated," to use Dr. Chalmers' word, in our great
towns. For instead of gradually abandoning the
stations whose support was forced upon it in 1843
by the necessities of its local adherents, the pas-
toral charges of the Free Church have by this
time nearly *doubled.*

In view of the openings which the future is
certain to bring to other communities, not necessarily in similar forms, nor, indeed, in religious
relations at all, the study of some of these various
channels and moulds as they were filled at once by

ono glowing enthusiasm, will always be important.
But for my purposes, and with a view to the suggestion that in the future the Free Church too
may hopefully hear itself called to a renewal of
self-sacrifice, and that not in one form but in
many, it is well to pause upon the results of the
half-century. Three years before its close the
Christian givings of this fragment of a poor
country, stripped in one day to the very bone,
had already amounted to more than twenty
millions. Yet during the first half of the half-
century they reached only about eight millions.
From time to time the figures have varied, as represented by the following, which gives the amount
for the opening year of each of its decades :—

1843	. . .	£363,871
1853	. . .	£289,670
1863	. . .	£343,626
1873	. . .	£511,084
1883	. . .	£628,222

The leap to the higher platform, which is
here so visible at one point, happened, strange to
say, just about the time when the last of the old
Disruption leaders was taken away, and the glory
of the separate communion they formed might
seem to have departed. But, in truth, it happened

—in accordance with all the deeper instincts of history—at the very time when that communion announced a resolve to sacrifice its long-prized separation, to refuse the bribe of re-establishment, and to claim henceforward part in the whole burdens of our country's future. And the result was in no respect strange. For the future of a country is to its Church "such a burden as wings are to a bird." The Free Church and its Sustentation Fund embody ideas important for Presbyterianism, and even for Congregationalism, in America and our Colonies and many a distant land. But their first duty is to their own country. And it seems to me that the time has at last come when the finance and other schemes of the Church of 1843 may frankly assume the aspect of provisional and experimental scaffolding— scaffolding in whose construction those now without should be consulted or considered as much as those within, because the Building which already rises behind it is one in which all Scottish Presbyterians have a right to dwell.

COLLEGE REMINISCENCES.

I.

EDINBURGH AND SIR WILLIAM HAMILTON.

EDINBURGH AND SIR WILLIAM HAMILTON.[1]

MOST of us, gentlemen, have passed our years of study in Edinburgh in comparative solitude and seclusion;—as strangers and sojourners, we pitched our tents in the shadow of the University. Not the less on that account did we love it, but rather the more—our fair foster-mother, the city of our adoption. Pleasant it was for our eager feet to wander along the streets of those two sister hills, with the green valley between them that once was the Nor'loch; those two hills that

[1] I reprint these utterances of a young man to young men (from a Valedictory Address in 1857 to the Dialectic Society of the University of Edinburgh), not because they are very wise or very conclusive. On the contrary, they are here, because their crude enthusiasm may the better recall to some readers the bridge—a break or a link in life as we choose to consider it—which so many men in Scotland and elsewhere have crossed on their way from the tranquil landscape of early youth to the problems and responsibilities of manhood.

stand opposed to each other like night and day—
stand opposed to each other, as if to picture to
young eyes the everlasting contrast and conflict of
the Old and the New. It was pleasant at all hours
—by day and by night. And there is one experi-
ence which I should like to recall, though I cannot
expect that others should fully sympathize with it.
I mean, rising in the early morning, before the
sun is up, and before the world is awake, and
going out into the midst of the mighty city, but
yesterday filled through all its streets with the
feverish flow of labour and of life, and now calm
and quiet and slumber-bound—none but yourself
awake—none but yourself is present—all others
are in another region, buried in unconsciousness,
or plunging through the abyss of dreams, ten
thousand miles away. You alone of all that city
are awake with God! You feel as if you were in
some enchanted land, wandering through a city
of the dead. I know nothing which starts so
many strange and mysterious feelings in the mind
—feelings neither to be chronicled nor explained.
But, in truth, this is not peculiar to town life.
Wherever we are, it is the tendency of the calm
blessedness of the early morning to fill the heart
with a strange sense of purity and peace; the
white light pouring in at the window recalls, we

know not how, the innocence of our half-forgotten
childhood—the humble trustful gaze forward, the
quiet earnest expectancy, of those of whom the
Lord of light said, "Of such is the kingdom of
heaven." To some these notions may appear
fantastic as well as visionary : the true students
know that the inner life is the true history of the
man—a history which is less influenced by elaborate reasonings than it may be by some casual
thought, which comes we know not whence, and
strikes us we know not how, perhaps in the
stillness of the early dawn, while the moon is yet
high in heaven, and the morning breaks upon the
sea. But let us return to Edinburgh, and to
Edinburgh during the day. No city deserves
sunshine better. But if we have taken · delight
in the architecture of Edinburgh, and favoured
the very stones thereof, still more have we enjoyed
those natural beauties with which she, above all our
cities, is invested and adorned; have marvelled at
the handiwork of that mighty Builder who reared
the Castle Rock, and laid the deep foundations of
Arthur's Seat. It is an affectation of the times
to speak with contempt of the pleasure derived by
town-born and town-bred citizens from the strips
and fragments of nature introduced into their
city. It is a mistake; and for myself, who am

not town-bred, but first looked upon nature from
the northern slope of a Ross-shire hill, I can
testify that I have had more pleasure in looking
out from my student lodgings upon a corner of
the Queen Street Gardens,—a few roods of tossing
foliage, half an acre of rich verdure into which
the eye can plunge and be refreshed,—than in
gazing over the forests waving on a thousand
hills. But Edinburgh is not obliged to content
herself with mere hints and morsels of natural
scenery. She is set by the hand of God where
the upheaved rock and the riven plain show
marks of the ancient war of conflagration and of
flood; it was the primeval fire that forged the
diadem of Arthur's Seat, and the sea monster has
guarded her young where now the stream of
humanity struggles through the Cowgate. That
early conflict has long since passed away; those
slopes and ridges have been rounded by the fingers
of slow creeping centuries; those valleys are green
with the verdure of unnumbered years: and yet
now, in the latter half of the nineteenth century,
when Scottish history is a tale of the past, we
have but to walk a few minutes from the old
Tolbooth of Edinburgh to find ourselves in the
midst of mountain scenery as graceful and as
bold, and in a retirement which is often as

profound, as if we stood amid the endless laby-
rinth of swelling hills between Blair-Atholo and
Braemar.   And in those days we used our inheritance well.   That was a happy hour when we sat
under the mighty precipice of the Castle Rock
and read Sir Thomas Browne on Urn Burial, or
Burton's Anatomy of Melancholy, or some other
rich and quaint book of the older time; and
looking up from the maze of well-woven words,
beheld that towering mass beetling above us, the
leaves of ivy creeping over its weather-stained
surface, and here and there a wallflower gleaming
in its savage clefts, while high above all frowned
those ancient battlements that guarded our Scottish kings.   And that was a white and a happy
day—one of our early Saturdays—when we laid
aside Horace and threw Homer away, and with
a volume of Shelley in the pocket, wandered off
round the green slopes of Arthur's Seat, while the
murmur of the city grew more and more distant
in our ears, and saw the outline of those glorious
Crags clear and sharp against the rich evening
sky, and returned not till the friendly night had
fallen upon men, and as we sauntered home with
weary foot and happy heart, the Old Town was
already gleaming like Pandemonium, a mass of
darkness blazing with unnumbered stars.

A youth passed amid sights and sounds such
as these was not an unhappy one, though it might
be studious and solitary. And yet it was not so
solitary after all. For can we ever forget the
charm of youthful friendship—the kindling intercourse of one mind with another, while iron
sharpened iron in the clash of contending intellects; and the stronger attraction of young hearts
welded to each other by a common interest in the
untrodden universe before? How near to us still
is that communion of thought and feeling nowhere
so lavishly enjoyed as in University life :—

> " When each by turns was guide to each,
>   And Fancy light from Fancy caught,
>   And Thought leapt out to wed with Thought
> Ere Thought could wed itself with Speech.
>
> " And all we met was fair and good,
>   And all was good that Time could bring,
>   And all the secret of the spring
> Moved in the chambers of the blood ;
>
> " And many an old philosophy
>   On Argive heights divinely sang,
>   And round us all the thicket rang
> To many a flute of Arcady."

How often thus did we walk under the green
beeches of Inverleith Row, or through the shelter-
ing laurels of the Botanic Gardens, or up the
Water of Leith, watching the noble arch above

us that spanned the dull stream below, or in some
quiet garden-like cemetery with the unquestioning
dead around, or up the old Hills of Braid, or the
green slopes of Corstorphine, or by the giant
trees of Craigmillar, or the broad avenue of the
Meadows, or along the murmuring shore of the
ancient sea. Many a profound question was laid
open in these walks of friendship :—

> " We reasoned high
> Of providence, fore-knowledge, will, and fate ;
> Fixed fate, free will, fore-knowledge absolute,
> And found no end, in wandering mazes lost.
> Of good and evil much we argued then,
> Of happiness and final misery,
> Passion, and apathy, and glory, and shame ! "

" Vain wisdom all, and false philosophy ! "
Perhaps it was—the harvest of those youthful
walks is not yet reaped : but we know and
remember how often, after a single hour's ramble
—after visiting many a corner of the universe,
and making many a track into chaos—we shook
hands with happy hearts, and returned to our
quiet rooms, wiser and better men.

    *   *   *   *   *

And here let us not forget him—whom some of
us never can forget—our departed Master : who,
while we were thirsting after knowledge, ranging
from object to object, and receiving innumerable

influences from every side, suddenly seized upon
our minds, and left his stamp on them for ever.
His stamp, I say : for amid that solid phalanx of
our contemporaries who have found their attendance on the philosophical classes in this University
an era in their lives, I believe there are few who
would not acknowledge that the secret of that
intellectual quickening was, not Sir William
Hamilton's philosophy, but Sir William Hamilton
himself. In estimating its nature and amount
we are not to think at all, or we are to make
comparatively little account, of the doctrines
which ˙ he held, the particular scientific or dogmatic statements which he laid before us. Some
of them we may possibly believe, others we may
probably deny ; [1] it is of very little consequence
to my present purpose whether we do the one or
the other. As was said of painters and Murillo,
Sir William Hamilton did more than make philo-
sophies, he made philosophers.

What the constituents of that powerful influence were we should find it impossible exhaustively
to state ; but some we may perhaps be able to

---

[1] Long before writing these grateful reminiscences—
indeed, before completing his second year in the philosophical class—the author had come to believe that Sir
William Hamilton's system was cracked from base to
summit.

recall. There was, in the first place, that feeling, which even his opening lectures were so well calculated to convey, the *sense of the dignity of the work* to which we were called. We who were but lately striplings and schoolboys were now invited, by a voice that stirred us like a trumpet, to enter into the very shrine and secret place of knowledge, to meet the art of arts and science of sciences,[1]—to handle the very elements of human thought—to deal with those great ideas which contain all others, those fundamental ideas which originate all others—to view the forms and relations of all things in the crystal globe of the soul, and the universe of intelligence mirrored in the microcosm of mind. What a sudden enlargement of vision was the result of this our work—what an amplitude of range, what an apparent boundlessness of prospect! We *felt* our minds expanding day after day, as we rose to the height of that great argument; till sometimes the young brain was hardly able to bear it, and I have gone home from those introductory lectures dizzy and reeling as if drunk with wine. And besides this feeling

---

[1] Sir William's class motto,—

" On Earth there is nothing great but Man ;
In Man there is nothing great but Mind."

of the nobility of our work, there was another,
distinct, though of a kindred nature, the awakened
consciousness of power. Nothing could be better
calculated to produce this than the exercise to
which whosoever entered Sir William Hamilton's
class must first give himself—the conquering of
that barricade of philosophical nomenclature,
that stubborn array of learned phraseology,
within which the master chose to hide and
half reveal his arguments and thoughts.   For
day by day as we gave ourselves to his work, and
as the work grew familiar to our hands, what
a change came over us! All our lives we had
been dealing with vague ideas, mumbling words
which had no distinct meaning in our minds or
which might have any meaning; seeing men like
trees walking, hazy thoughts, nebulous concep-
tions, misty imaginations, muddy arguments; now,
point by point and part by part, all things grew
clear before our eyes: we used no word ourselves
that was not limited and defined; we believed no
word of others that did not present a distinct idea
to our minds—the chaos of thinking became a
cosmos of thoughts.   And as each idea was distinct, so each statement was a distinct union of
two ideas themselves clear and defined; everything in the universe dovetailed into everything

else; all things were united—nothing was confounded. It was a wonderful discipline for the young mind: and it was more than a discipline; for it gave us at the same time confidence and courage. We now knew what we said; we might hope hereafter to say what we knew. For, as we then came thoroughly to believe, no one has a right to say what he thinks unless he first thinks what he says. And now all things were before us—all questions, all theories, all speculations, all opinions—all products of human thought were in our hands—to analyse, to sift, to search, to disintegrate into their component elements, to reunite to their original sources, to pull down and to rear up, to build and to destroy. It was a large privilege for young men; and we claimed it to the utmost. With such an organon in our hands, and with such a stimulus in our hearts, what was there that we might not accomplish, what was there that we might not attempt? Confident we were—too confident; sceptical and scrutinizing, daring and dogmatic: yet, let us hope, all was not in vain. The dogmatism of young men gets rubbed away in their after intercourse with the world; their scepticism is repressed by the craving for something stable to cling to amid the buffetings of life and the mysteries of time;

and there remains, or should remain, the sharp and searching eye, and the stout and strong heart. And one thing more, which may be recalled as the last ingredient in the influence exercised by Sir William Hamilton—*the love of truth.* " What is truth? said jesting Pilate, and would not stay for a reply." We stayed for a reply—we waited at wisdom's door—waited long and well. The first effect of that blast of analysis was to strip off from us all our old notions and prejudices like leaves from the trees in autumn. " Philosophy," said Sir William, " demands the renunciation of all previous opinions; " and when we came to examine our opinions, when we became conscious of the vagueness, shallowness, and ambiguity of them all, the hearsay and second-hand nature of many of them, and the hollowness and insincerity of some, it was with no doubtful mind that we obeyed the call, and threw them all aside. But if we did so, it was not in the spirit of scepticism or indifference to truth: we surrendered our beliefs that we might seek the true belief; we flung our bread upon the waters that we might find it after many days! For at this time there awoke in our minds that feeling which is at all times latent in the breast of every human being, but which now became a passion—a hunger of the

soul—the love of *truth*—truth, first good, first fair
—not of an age, of a sect, or of a school, but, like
its author, " id ipsum, et id ipsum, et id ipsum,"
—unchangeable and divine. " O Veritas, Veritas,
quam intime etiam tum animi mei medullae suspi-
rabant tibi ; . . . ut non illam aut illam sectam,
sed ipsam quaecunque esset sapientiam ut diligerem,
et quaererem, et adsequerer, et tenerem, atque
amplexarer, fortiter excitabar et accendebar et
ardebam." [1]

* * * * *

But there is one influence, derived not so much
from our studies, as from the circumstances amid
which they were carried on, which is felt with full
force only by those who have not passed their
early days in the city, but have come up to the
University from the country. That is a startling
transition in many respects—in none perhaps
more than this—that the life of great cities, seen
for the first time, awakened in the soul a feeling
of which it was hardly conscious before—the idea
of Humanity ; of the race, with its destinies and
hopes. In the country life is isolated ; we see it
in details, we are conversant only with individuals. It is when we come to town that the full

[1] Augustine, *The Confessions*

import of that sorrowful phrase of modern times,
"the masses," breaks upon our minds. I have
spoken already of the various points from which
we have contemplated this fair town of Edinburgh; but what to my mind always appears the
most interesting of them all has yet to be mentioned. It is this—to stand upon the south side
of the Calton Hill, and turning your face towards
those noble Salisbury Crags, to look across the
deep valley of humanity that lies between, and
listen to the multitudinous murmur that rises
from its crowded homes and swarming streets.
Nature is fair on either side—the slopes before
us are green as the fields of paradise—but how is
it with man? From that abyss at our feet, filled
and brimming over with immortal souls, what is
the voice that calls to us? It is the voice of
labour—of grinding dull unmitigated toil—sometimes of youth without innocence and of age
without honour—of virtuous poverty, struggling
in vain to rise above the evils of its lot—of
poverty not virtuous, sinking under the double
load of misfortune and of crime. No wonder that
such a sight, day by day before our eyes, burned
deep into our souls the sense of the evils of our
race. It was the same old story of sorrow—never
ending, ever beginning; how, age after age, the

many toil for the few, and the few despise the
many ; how while empires have flourished and
decayed, the mass of mankind have at all times
had the same destiny, living out their life on the
verge of destitution, with deep slow sorrows and
few joys, and a bitter blast blowing on them from
the shore of death ;—how, while poverty has been
the curse of the poor, satiety has been the curse
of the rich, and vanity and vexation of spirit the
lot of both ; and how generation after generation
have looked and longed for something better in
the future, till hope deferred has made the world's
heart sick. And what a stimulus was this to us
--to us, who loved truth, and believed in the truth
which we loved. It was now no abstract notion—
no beautiful idea of truth which we sought ; we
sought for that which should regenerate the world.
Surely error must be essentially weak, and truth
must conquer in the end : " Magna est Veritas, et
prevalebit ! " And yet——

*　　*　　*　　*　　*

And now for the future.

Gentlemen, shall we ever come to regret those
early years ? Will the time ever come to us, as
it has come to many wiser and better than we,
when the visions of our youth shall have faded

away, and have given place to the maxims and
practices of the world? Shall we who have
loved truth with a disinterested and a passionate
love—shall we be contented with a conformity
to the hollow respectabilities of place, of station,
and of time, with dogmas on our lips which we
suspect to be false, with truths in advance of us
which we are too cowardly to meet? Shall we
whose hearts have burned within us at the sight
of the evils of humanity, the oppressions that are
done under the sun, the sore travail of this
burdened and groaning world—shall we ever
come into a state of contented indifference to the
hopes and the destinies of our race; because perhaps we have a secure and a comfortable lot, while
our brethren are struggling around? Or shall
we who have loved virtue, who have longed
after the καλὸν and the αγαθόν, the good and
the true; who have sought earnestly for some
security by which we might keep our garments
white and our lamps undimmed amid the
drifting storms of life—shall we come to look
upon all that as a too fervid dream, the enthusiasm of youth, which it is well for youth to have,
but which the man cannot afford to cherish or to
believe? Such things may be—such things have
been: it is well that we should keep the possibility

of them before our view. We may not indeed descend to that mournful and extreme contrast to the better days of youth which Alfred Tennyson gives in his strange "Vision of Sin." We may still preserve a formal allegiance to truth, a decent respect for philanthropy, and an outward attachment to virtue ; while the world has wholly eaten away the core and kernel of our life. We *may* come gradually, and little by little, to admire riches, to prostrate ourselves before external greatness, to "call the proud happy," to barter our inward peace for the advantage of the hour or the applause of the multitude—to regard success in life as a thing worthy of our exertions and our hopes. And we may ere long learn—our life may be toned down to it—to make up our minds to a certain modicum of truth which we think it convenient to carry about with us, but which we do not find it necessary vividly to realize, or earnestly to obey, or loyally to follow out—we who in other days strode onwards into chaos, and buffeted the darkness, and struggled and strove for light, and saw through the mists of error and doubt the fair face of truth beckoning us on, and followed her with weary foot and dauntless heart far into the waste places of intelligence. When those evil days come, and the years draw nigh, in

12

which we shall say, I have no pleasure in them,
it may be not without advantage for us to recall
how, in the earlier dawn, we lived a life at the
University of Edinburgh,

  "Beneath the good how far, but far above the great."

COLLEGE REMINISCENCES.

II.

EDINBURGH AND SOME OF ITS CHURCHMEN.

179

EDINBURGH AND SOME OF ITS CHURCHMEN.

THERE have been nations, or at least there have been times in the history of nations, when the Universities influenced the youth and the Church did not. It was not so in Edinburgh in the time from which the above too youthful utterances have been disinterred. One reason may have been that the part of the Church which was under the strongest pressure of un-equal legislation, never thought of abandoning its own fair share in that higher education which, in so far as it is university, is European rather than national. When the grey hairs of Dr. Chalmers and Dr. Welsh were excluded from the Edinburgh Senatus, the Divinity students who, with them, adhered to the Assembly's pledge, were also excluded from their share in the private benefactions left them by their Scottish ancestors. And for fifty years both exclusions have been continued. But the immediate effect of this cruel hardship was to make it certain in 1843 that the Free Church would have an academical side of its own. And the remote result was to group outside the University walls a number of men whose intellectual stature in those days attracted youth, even when it was most disposed to distrust the Christian Church and all its claims. Of those venerable forms, strangely enough, the one which now most abides with me was the most eccentric of all—the man whom his students used to call Rabbi Duncan. Not that he was a Jew ; but his flowing beard, flowing garments, retreating hat, glittering eye, and great guttural tones, instantaneously suggested that this must be the ancient Wanderer himself—*Der Ewige Jude*—on his polyglot way across the world from the wall of China, or escaped into our modern age from the remote and spectral corridors of Talmudic lore. Where he had really come from, however, was the house of an Aberdeen shoemaker, where the sickly boy, consumed with a double passion for learning and speculation, was early heard to pray, " O that God would spare me till I get on the red cloakie ! " But even after he assumed the coveted undergraduate garb, the youth might be seen to stand in

the granite street in utter absence of mind, and
" wrap it around him, asking, with a shiver,
' What, after all, are we in this world for ? ' "
till after three years of " Spinozism, Pantheism,
and Atheism," that grand old moderate, Dr.
Mearns, brought him on so far as to think that
there *might* be a God, and " I danced on the brig
of Dee for delight, though I feared that He might
damn me." And many more wanderings followed,
with at least two mental cataclysms, before the
wonderful old man was able to say, " I am a
philosophical sceptic, who have taken refuge in
theology," or to explain, in snuff-burdened solilo-
quy, to those who pressed him on what the refuge
was, " I am first a Christian, next a Catholic,
then a Calvinist, fourth a Pædobaptist, and fifth a
Presbyterian ; and I cannot reverse this order."
The most helpless and unworldly of men—at first
appearance a mere scarecrow of erudition—he
was soon recognised, even by us who had been
passionate followers of Sir William Hamilton, as
ruling an equal domain of learning, but with a
more commanding intellectual sway. Yet he
wrote no lectures ; he published no books. His
realm was colloquial. But in that realm it seemed
as if Pascal had shuffled into the sandals of Soc-
rates, and walked up and down our Edinburgh

streets, with large utterance of response to the
inquiring youth around.[1]

But the Church held its own against more
imposing forces than the exclusive University.
The men who formed its leaders in 1843 have
been often recognised as a group of statesmen of
extraordinary power, even when compared—and
by men who could compare both from within—
with the Cabinet and Parliamentary leaders of
the august Victorian age.[2]   The greatest of them
all, Dr. Chalmers, I was just too late to see; but
his voice yet speaks, and the last volume of his
life remains to this day the best narrative of that
struggle with the State in which the famous

[1] To get a complete view of Dr. John Duncan you
must take his utterances from Professor Knight's *Colloquia;* his history from Principal Brown's *Memorials;* and
his finer characteristics from Dr. Moody Stuart's *Recollections.*

[2] "The best and greatest men I have ever known."
Letter by the Duke of Argyll in 1874.

"You have now been a good many years in Parliament," a friend said to Mr. Murray Dunlop before 1870,
"and have heard many debates. How do they impress
you as compared with the Assembly debates before the
Disruption?" He at once replied, with great emphasis,
"I never heard anything like those Assembly debates.
We have no men in Parliament like those men. There
is no man in the House that approaches Cunningham."—
Cunningham's Life, p. 483.

Conservative Churchman was driven by conscience, in opposition to all his prepossessions, to take the lead.[1] Nor shall I say anything on Dr. Thomas Guthrie, of all men whom I have known the most eloquent, and with far more power than even Chalmers over the springs of laughter and of tears. But there are two whom I should like to characterise; for one of them was to the end of his life the most authoritative man in the Free Church, while the other was then, and long after, its foremost preacher and the leader of its General Assembly.

Dr. William Cunningham, Principal of the New College in succession to Dr. Chalmers, had great learning, and had along with it those higher qualities which in Scotland are supposed to be necessary for a theologian. But of all men to whom I have ever listened, in the Senate, on the platform, or at the Bar, he was the weightiest debater. And recalling at present only this aspect of the man, we naturally ask, first, What did he look like? He was a sluggish giant, with length of trunk added on to length of limb, so

---

[1] It is perhaps professional partiality that makes me add, to Dr. Hanna and to a greater writer, Hugh Miller, a third classic in Lord Cockburn, whose *Journal* is largely devoted to the same topic.

that the swing and roll of his gait came to be like those of a seventy-four gun-ship. And the shaggy head which surmounted this portentous person generally looked out upon you with a mixture of mildness and menace—present mildness and post-poned or possible menace—which you came before long to think characteristic of the man morally, and even mentally. For Dr. Cunningham united in himself two excellences, very rarely found in combination in the same mind, and almost never in such an extraordinary degree. On the one hand, there was a singular moderation, calmness, and common sense; a deliberative honesty of mind, which rejected rash exaggerations and re-fused hasty conclusions, and which demanded always to see the true state of the whole case, content with nothing less, and desirous of nothing more. In order to attain this there was a reserve of judgment and suspense of-thought, impressing those who came in contact with him with the strongest admiration of his judicial impartiality and integrity ; and this self-poised uprightness of intellect, and freedom from bias and mental par-tisanship, made men resort to him to the very end of his life as a counsellor on whom almost absolute reliance could be placed. But along with this admirable moderation of mind, and in strange

contrast with it, must be placed the still more
notorious fact, that Dr. Cunningham was, characteristically and by life-long choice, a fighting
theologian, and that his whole writing and speaking were characterised by a vigour and even a
vehemence of controversy such as we very seldom
meet. Now the *modus operandi* of such a mind,
the way in which it brings into interaction the
two parts of its nature, must be peculiar and
noteworthy. The calmness of Dr. Cunningham's
deliberation, and the vehemence of his action,
were no doubt such as to seem almost inconsistent
with each other. But the point of junction
between the two, the hinge on which they rested
and turned, was to be found in his own constant
and characteristic phrase, the *status quæstionis*.
It was this that he sought in deliberation; this
that he urged in action. Up to the point of
having satisfied himself what the true question
to be decided was, he was wise, moderate, and
comprehensive; but, when his conscience and intellect were sufficiently and clearly persuaded as
to *the truth on the question*, he seized upon this as
a battle-axe, and hurled through the press of men
with all the weight of his nature. It was first
Argus with his hundred eyes; and then Briareus,
all his eyes shut up, and all his leaded hands set

free.   Hence resulted one striking characteristic
of Dr. Cunningham's controversial appearances,
a continual and powerful iteration. He had made
up his mind (and generally with an unerring instinct) what the true question was, how it should
be stated, and how answered; and the question
and answer he put with matchless power.   But if
any one wished the question to be put in some
other form, or the answer to be given from some
other point of view, Dr. Cunningham was not the
man to do it.   His large, and sluggish, and honest
nature had had too much trouble already with it
lightly to alter his point of view; he had come
deliberately, and with the widest comprehensive-
ness, to his conclusion ; and what it behoved him
now to do was to urge that upon other men.
This was his manner all through the Scottish
Church controversies, and in every other in which
he was engaged.   He hit the nail on the head at
first, and drove it deep; if any one objected that
was not the true nail, he simply hit it again ; and
if any one still brought forward reasons, *he hit it
again* with a sledge-hammer vigour and resonance.
He was not a man of intellectual resource ; he
was not excursive ; he was not discursive ; he was
not even progressive ; he swung in his orbit,
movens non promovens.   He was not given to

reasoning in public; his logic was all bestowed
(it is, perhaps, all that logic can do) upon clearing
and defining his position; but he did this with
a breadth, a strength, a manliness, and, above
all, a convincingness, which impressed men far
more than the utmost ingenuity in debate. My
favourite comparison for Dr. Cunningham used
to be to a man-of-war swinging lazily at anchor
with all its guns double-shotted. But, if I were
to describe his manner in action, it must rather be
likened to the straightforward proceeding of that
American vessel which shortly after his death
startled the world by crashing head foremost into
the ribs of its adversary, and then drawing off to
run straight at it again, and crash into it conclusively once more.

No one could be a greater contrast to Dr.
Cunningham than was Dr. Robert Smith Candlish. Discursive, excursive, expansive, and explo-
sive, his slender and nervous frame was scarcely
big enough to contain that

> "Fiery soul, which, working out its way,
> Fretted the pigmy body to decay,
> And o'er-informed its tenement of clay."

Only the great forehead and the large lustrous
and woman-like eyes gave assurance of those

mental and moral gifts whose combination made
him, ever since 1843, or at all events after the
death of Dr. Chalmers in 1847, the leader of the
Free Church.   No doubt in a free republic the
leader follows quite as much as he leads, and
within certain limits ought to do so.   But to sustain such relations to any of our ecclesiastical
bodies as this man so long did, requires strong
convictions and profound sympathies to begin
with, great and varied gifts directed by a sleepless
energy and zeal, and high and disinterested moral
qualities in addition to all.   These and many other
qualifications Dr. Candlish eminently had.   A
consummate man of business, and a born lawyer,
on the one hand, with a genius for elucidation and
extrication such as no man left behind him in
Scotland has at all possessed; he was, on the
other hand, an orator of the Ciceronian style and
class, full, clear, voluminous, and sweeping, but
with, in addition, a power of sudden outburst and
conflagration whose effect was extraordinary.
But memories which draw back to years at college
will cluster specially round Dr. Candlish as a
preacher.   For, however much other intellectual
influences in those days attracted us, we were
conscious of no descent when the day came for the
halls of knowledge to be closed, and the doors of

prayer to be opened. Even when the first dazzle
of novelty had worn off, and we came to discern
the defects of his qualities, we came to love him,
not less, but more. It was perhaps, indeed, he
who loved the preacher best who could best put
his finger upon his characteristic faults and excellencies, as I recall both to-day.

On the one side, you had the excessive subtlety
of gratuitous analysis; the incapacity for stating
a doctrine simply and by itself, without under-
founding it by some metaphysical or theological
theory, or buttressing it by some unexpected argument or skilful analogy, or at least disjoining and
discriminating it from everything that it was not,
and might by any chance be supposed to be; the
viciously antithetic form of thought, which made
the speaker sway continually from side to side of
his argument, like a ship rolling in the tide; the
logical sword-play, which flashed now on this side
and now on that, cutting the air, but dividing
neither soul nor spirit; the hard rhetorical ring
and resonance, which were never wanting, even
when the thought and feeling had for the moment
sunk to a minimum; the text twisted in order to
have the pleasure of putting it straight again;
the ingenious explanation that explained nothing;
the unreasonable reason for what required no

reason at all; and the admirable defence that made you doubt the doctrine defended.

On the other side, there were the many excellencies of which these vices were but the occasional and wanton excess—the vast amount of theological material, and the perfect mastery shown in handling and using it all; the victorious ease with which difficulties were surmounted and knots untied; the lavish intellectual energy poured forth upon every subject and every occasion; the wonderful perspicacity which expounded so much that was obscure, and unravelled all that was complicated, and united all that was distant or diverse; the confluence of contributory argument from remote heights of thought and philosophy, so that, for younger hearers especially, we might almost parody with regard to Dr. Candlish the compliment paid to a lady a hundred years ago, and say that to sit under that pulpit was " a liberal education; " the simple and strong grasp with which, amid his exuberant intellectual discursiveness, he held the plain and central truths of the gospel, and the enviable power with which, after soaring in the first part of his discourse through dim metaphysical heights, and doubtful metaphysical theories, he invariably swooped down towards the close, and fastened on the con-

science and heart of his hearers ; the keen practical instinct and quick practical sympathies that
made his sermons spread so effectively over the
whole breadth of human life ; the admirable skill
in detecting motives, and dissecting feelings, and
dealing with the will, and sending the light of
divine truth clear and strong through all the
intricacies and tortuosities of the inner man ; the
clear, full, flexible, and melodious voice, the com-
pass and distinctness of which gave the idea of
the "trumpet talking" of the Apocalypse, and
ranged from a clear-heard and persuasive whisper
to the peal of crashing and reverberating indignation—all these, and still more, the almost child-
like simplicity and sincerity and single-hearted-
ness and self-forgetfulness, which in this case were
found to be consistent with a mental ingenuity
tending to deceive both himself and others ; so
that the best summing up of the characteristics of
Dr. Candlish as a preacher might be found in the
verdict passed by an acute female critic upon his
whole course, " An honest heart behind a subtle
understanding."

Dr. Candlish's subtlety of understanding led
him sometimes in the pulpit to hang too great
weights upon straining wires. Dr. Cunningham's
massiveness of learning led him habitually to

speak of theologians in the past as having "conclusively determined and practically exhausted"
theology, and so to leave little room for devout
inquiry or devout speculation in the present.
Both failings tended to produce a dangerous revulsion in young minds, even of those who loved as
well as admired the men. But as Churchmen,
and in dealing with the questions to which most
of these pages are devoted, it did not seem to me
that either of these great leaders showed any
narrowness. As Scottish statesmen they stood
on a height, and looked all around and far in
advance. The only occasion on which I conferred
with them both on matters of importance—of
course long after student days—was in relation to
what was then known as the "Cardross Case."
And I remember how surprised I was to find the
two veterans of the Spiritual Independence battle
apparently not so much anxious for the independence of the Church—*that* they seemed to
think the Church would take care of itself, as in
this particular case it had with great emphasis
done—both seemed at least equally interested in
the dignity of the Bench and the obligation of
the civil laws to deal justly with all "patri-
monial" questions, the decision of which the documents of 1843 make in all circumstances not the

right only of the Civil Courts, but their absolute
duty. And with regard to the question of Church
union and the yet unfulfilled future of Scotland,
both of them were wide-seeing and far-seeing.
Dr. Chalmers, so late as 1847, had nothing to
offer to the House of Commons but the hard *sum-
mum jus* of the Free Church claim of 1843.[1] But
both Cunningham and Candlish had learned in
that very crisis to look forward to a solution more
harmonious and brotherly, not only as between
churches, but as between their members and the
citizens outside. Through their influence it was
provided that the adhesion to be required to those
documents of 1843, from officials of the Free
Church, should be not to its minor claims of resti-
tution, just as these might be; but to its more
central principles, central in the present and hope-
ful for the future. Dr. Cunningham, even in the
beginning of 1844, formally declared, to the largest
body of Presbyterians in the world, that there was

[1] " Is there any prospect of a reunion ? " " I think that
a restoration is possible, but not in the way of a reunion.
... We must, of course, provide for the perfect integrity
of our own ecclesiastical principles, and I do not see how
that can be done, except by the Legislature adopting the
Free Church as the Establishment, and then leaving us to
deal with the ministers of the Established Church as so
many ecclesiastical delinquents."—*Memoirs*, IV., 597.

no chance of the harmonious action of the Scottish
Free Churches in the future being disturbed by
any acceptance on the part of his own Church of
State proposals.[1]   And his latest Assembly speech
(which Dr. Candlish, then Moderator, said at once
was as powerful as any delivered in the great ante-
Disruption days) was a defence, on still more
explicit grounds, of the incorporating union of the
Free Church and the United Presbyterian Church
in Australia.   For Dr. Candlish himself it was
reserved—and in his own view it was the highest
honour of that brilliant and beautiful life now so

[1] Upon two grounds. 1. That the improbability of any
existing State offering assistance and support to a Church
on terms and conditions with which it would be lawful
for a Church of Christ to comply, "was so great as practically to amount, in our judgment, to an impossibility :"
and 2. "That even if the State were to make to us proposals which, viewed in themselves, involved nothing that
was in our apprehension inconsistent with the full recognition of all our rights and liberties as a Church of Christ,
we would attach very great weight in deciding upon them,
to the consideration of the way and manner in which our
acceptance or refusal would bear on our relation to the
other Churches of Christ ; as there is good reason to
believe that the maintenance of a strict relation between
the Churches of Christ in a community would have a far
more important bearing upon the interests of religion and
the welfare of Christ's people than anything the civil
power could do."—*Life of Cunningham*, 514.

soon to close—to propose the same union between
the parent Churches in his native land. He did
it with the active concurrence of Mr. Murray
Dunlop, the author of the documents of 1843, as
well as of Dr. Robert Buchanan, the historian of
the Free Church, and of Sir Henry Moncreiff, its
lawyer and divine; and when the unreadiness of
many members of their Church made the post-
ponement of the union necessary, he recorded
their common conviction, that its principles demanded and ensured that it shall yet be carried
out. Yet there were even then some outside the
Assembly, like Dr. Blaikie within it, who, while
equally convinced of this, thought also that the
intermediate position of a Scottish Church brings
with it a twofold burden of duty, and that union
with one side might be premature until overtures
had been made to the other.

RECONSTRUCTION.

AS URGED UPON FREE CHURCHMEN IN
' 1868 AND 1878.

❧

RECONSTRUCTION

URGED UPON FREE CHURCHMEN IN ·1868.[1]

NOTHING is more plain than that for the next twenty years the extent to which the Court will respect the alleged essential Church rights of such a body as the Free Church, will depend chiefly on how far that body takes up the essential position of *the* Church—takes it up, I mean, broadly, obviously, and effectively ; and also effects an unmistakable union with other bodies throughout the world, whose Church standing is already acknowledged by the law, like those just mentioned in America. How such a Church standing is to be made manifest, and in particular by what methods such a Church unity is to be wrought out, is a question so large that it may be gladly left to the members of the Free Church itself, especially since the pamphlet of Dr. Rainy. But

[1] From two letters to *The Daily Review* of dates 13th and 29th of February, 1868, in response to five papers by Sir Henry W. Moncreiff, Bart., in that journal, reviewing a volume on " The Law of Creeds in Scotland."

there are many things connected with this question not yet brought up; and almost every way
of dealing with it would seem to me to be tolerable, except the unconscientious way, which refuses
to deal with it at all. For example, I do not
think the duty of the Free Church is at all yet
exhausted towards the Established Church; and
the present revival in it of the old anti-patronage
agitation is fitted to remind us of this powerfully.
That agitation may be beside the mark, so far as
questions with other Churches are concerned; and
it is certainly opposed to the suggestions of worldly
wisdom as regards the security and quiet of the
Establishment itself. But all the more on that
account do I admire and love the unselfish zeal
and Christian instinct which prompts men to do,
at all risks, what it seems to them they *may* do,
and which somewhere and somehow shall not lose
its reward. It is, indeed, at least as impossible for
a Free Churchman as for a Voluntary to go back
into the Establishment, as Establishment has
latterly been defined in Scotland; and patronage
has nothing to do with the matter; and it is not
the Established Church but the State that has
now power to go even a single step in the direction
of lifting the real bar. Yet, in these days of
startling changes, is there anything impossible in

the idea that all parties may soon again form one
Church; that the State, which is and has been
the great divider, may take the needed step towards restoring to unity that Church which has
the same anti-Erastian doctrine in its standards
and the same history to look back upon? And,
even if the State does nothing, and the Free
Church, and United Presbyterian Church, and
Cameronian Church find themselves shut up to
put an end to their present state of schism and
separation, is the Free Church not bound before
doing so solemnly to fall back on her protests of
1843, to point out that these are founded not on
her imagined rights as Church of Scotland, but on
the inalienable rights of conscience which are
common to every Church of Christ, and on this
ground to publish and press these once more on
the minds of men generally; and, in particular, to
offer union with itself to the Established Church
on this ground—(an offer which no part of that
Church could think ridiculous, if it knew that it
was immediately to be followed by the union of all
the branches of the old Kirk of Scotland)—until
so at last, having finally exhausted its historical
responsibility, it merges itself in the better and
higher name? I suspect something of this sort
will be found necessary to satisfy not only the

imagination, but the conscience of the Free
Church, before the union with the other Free
Presbyterians can be consummated.

*   *   *   *   *

In considering the law of creeds in Scotland, it
was necessary to go over the whole ground of the
relation of the Churches; and as the result of that
review I hold :—

1. That the Free Church, the United Presbyterian Church, and the Reformed Presbyterian
Church, *are already* essentially one Church, and
that any attempt, whether by perpetuating separate organisations or otherwise, to divide them,
is an attempt to destroy the only Presbyterian
Church (unestablished) to which any Scotchman
owes any allegiance whatever.

2. That the attempt since 1843 on the part of
any one of these Churches, and particularly of the
Free Church, to set itself up in permanent separation, and claim to be the " Church of Scotland" in
any other sense than that in which it acknowledges
them to be so too (*i.e.*, the sense of " the Church
of Christ in Scotland"), is not only schismatic and
sectarian, but is destructive of the only principle
on which it claims to be free, or on which it can
honestly maintain a separate existence from the
Establishment.

3. That this is the only ground on which the whole contendings of the Church party in the Establishment, from 1833 to 1843, can be defended, or even rendered intelligible; and that any attempt to base the Free Church on constitutional ground peculiar to itself, instead of upon the general ground of conscience common to it with the older branches of the Kirk, would unweave backwards every plea used by it in the Law Courts or Legislature, even to the first Auchterarder case, would prove its whole great argument illogical and false, and make those who then rested on that argument martyrs by mistake.

4. That this is as recognisable on the side of the State and the Court as on that of the Church. For the strongest ground of the judges was that whatever other rights the Church might have, it was nevertheless and also the Church of Scotland; and if it is so *essentially*—*i.e.*, if it was *essentially* connected with the State of Scotland—there can be little doubt that the whole argument of the Court was right, and that their proceedings, however harsh, were but the carrying out of what it was their duty to do. And, on the other hand, it is now not only a doctrine of the Law Courts, but a doctrine of the British Constitution adopted by the State (the adoption of which is acknowledged and

founded on in the Protest of 1843), that all Church Establishment has been, will be, and seemingly in its nature must be, on the principle of subordination of the Church to the State, and that therefore, as I put it formerly, all meddling with Establishments on the part of those holding the old principles of the Kirk was a mistake—a mistake of three hundred years' duration.

5. That this truth as to the essential position of the Church came out especially when near the Disruption, and is embodied in the Claim of Right and in the Protest; which base the Church, not on the constitutional rights conceded to it by the State, or on anything claimable by it as a State Church, but on the inalienable duty of the Church to perform its own functions.

6. How, then, can the Free Church, on coming out from the Establishment in 1843, do anything *else* than unite with its Presbyterian brethren outside? It is in an essentially intermediate and transitive position. It cannot go back into the Establishment. That course is not in its power. But it may unite with its elder, and perhaps, on the whole, purer sisters, and with the present members of the Established Church, to form the old Kirk as it was in its beginning—in the words of the greatest of Scotchmen, "to reduce again to the

eyes and knowledge of men the reverend face of that primitive and apostolic Kirk " in Scotland which he laboured to build up.   It is not a matter of option with it whether it will do this.   It is a matter of necessity—of necessity and of conscience. If the Free Church sinks in the next generation into a separate sect among the Non-established Churches, I must repeat what I ventured to say before, that the defection from it of the youth of Scotland, though certain, will not be the worst issue.   That, indeed, will certainly happen ; it is not a remote result.   But can any patriot wish, can any Christian desire, that such a cause should be followed by any other or better result ?   While, on the other hand, seeing the youth of Scotland are taught, what scarcely any one seems to venture to deny, that the three negotiating Churches are all members of the Old Church of Scotland, will not the result of the process towards union be, in the first place, a deep satisfaction of conscience on this perplexing subject of the Church, and in the next place, the awakening of an infinite pride in the remembrance of all the sacred past, which, like the setting sun kindling even the Eastern sky, shall become a great hope for the future in the hearts and on the faces of the young ?

RECONSTRUCTION

URGED UPON FREE CHURCHMEN IN 1878.[1]

YEAR by year, as I read foreign and contemporary history, your hereditary claim of right is more and more acknowledged as conclusive—acknowledged by scholars and thinkers abroad, as well as at home by historians and statesmen so various in their sympathies as Mr. Tytler and Lord Macaulay, the Duke of Argyll and Mr. Gladstone.

And yet, while your right to be simply replaced in your position is more and more admitted by others, it is in that form less and less pressed by yourselves. The change implies a generous paradox, and a self-abnegation wholly worthy of you; but it has hitherto been founded very much upon mere instinct. I desire to-night to probe the foundations of principle upon which I believe it to rest, and to suggest that we are now called to still higher developments. And, in order to this, I

[1] From Lecture in Free St. George's, Edinburgh, on "Church and State in Scotland," 1878.

take your Claim of Right of 1842. Like those
high authorities, I bow before it. I admit that
it is valid and conclusive against the present Established Church. But I put the question, Is it
equally valid to the exclusion of the rest of Scotland, to the exclusion of the other Presbyterians
outside of you? I do not ask you whether you
will use it to exclude them, or whether you will
ever use it at all in your own interests apart from
theirs. I know your intentions on this subject—
your declared intentions—are wholly generous,
and absolutely unsectarian and national. But
I leave the matter of generosity, and I raise the
prior question of right. What are your rights,
and what are theirs, in the matter? Now, from
the first day on which I was able to form an
opinion on this great subject, I have always held
that you have no right whatever, either in law or
in justice, against your brethren in Scotland who
maintain with you the independence of the
Church. Take the Cameronians in 1690. They
held that the Revolution Settlement in its bearing
on previous legislation was ambiguous, and might
be construed in an Erastian sense against the
Church, and so they thought it not safe to go into
it. You thought it safe to go into it; and, in
1843, the Courts and the Parliament construed

14

that Settlement and all the older Acts, elabor-
ately, solemnly, and repeatedly—on their own
merits, too, and apart from the question of
patronage—in precisely the sense which was
dreaded so long ago. The Cameronians were
right, and you were wrong : whose claim is a
Claim of Right? Take Gillespie in 1752. He
seceded and formed the Relief Church, because the
Assembly ordered him to take a part in intruding
a minister upon a reclaiming congregation—precisely what you refused to do in 1843 when
ordered, not now by the Church, but by the State.
You are both in the same boat ; but whose is the
stronger right? whose is the prior claim? The
truth is, there is a complete solidarity in this
matter among all the branches of the Old Kirk
of Scotland; and I am far from excluding any
members of the Church established who claim
their share in our common heritage. There is
a constitutional and vital unity already existing among our Scottish Free Churches, deeper
than any blending of organisations; a unity
which we all feel as a moral fact, and which
some of us have been long prepared to base
upon historical principles. Never once have
I been present when your Assembly stood up to
" pray that Jerusalem may have peace and

felicity," without seeming to behold the walls fall asunder, and the roofs expand, and a greater house silently rise, to receive the invisible multitude of our Scottish faith and blood. And that vision was no baseless fabric : it rested, I believe, on a logical foundation, and it leads to a practical result. I hold that your Claim of Right, if put so as to exclude the others—if founded solely on what is historically peculiar to yourselves—is not worth the paper on which it is written. But if your claims are founded on what is common and essential to the ancient Kirk—if they are put by you, not for yourselves alone, but, as you are well entitled to put them, vicariously or representatively for the rest—then I believe that such a claim contains in it at this hour the destinies of Scotland, and will yet receive the homage of the world.

For myself, I shall never cease to maintain that what rights you of the Free Church have, the United Presbyterians and Reformed Presbyterians have also, on essentially the same grounds. And I am not in the least moved by the consideration that many of the former are theoretical Voluntaries, and that they hold the opinion that there should be no connection of the Scottish Church and State. The question is not of their

opinions, but of their rights; and not how they
will use their rights, but whether they as well as
you possess them. I have never been able to see
the difficulty on this point, and I think any
puzzle as to it springs from confusion of ideas.
It may or may not have been right for Scotland
to give privileges to the Presbyterian Church at
all, but in point of fact it has given them; and
that historical fact raises the historical question—
if you like, it creates the question—Who has a
right to those privileges, and who has dispossessed
the owners of the right? It may be a question
whether a Faculty of Advocates ought to exist in
Scotland; but, so long as it exists, I have no right
to usurp my learned friend's wig in order to
appear with it even in the Court of Teinds, far
less in order to sell it in an English pawnshop.
It may be a question whether John Knox should
have accepted any State Endowment instead of
sticking to his original idea of a Sustentation Fund
by the people; but that can never interfere with
the other question, whether he accepted those
endowments for Dr. Cook and Dr. Blair to the
exclusion of Ralph Erskine and Thomas Chalmers
—or whether the dust stirred in his grave, when
an English majority in 1843 wrenched his endowments from the protesting hands of our repre-

sentatives in Parliament. Yes, the question of
right is wholly independent of the theoretical
inquiry whether there ought to have been a State
Church at all, and still more of the inquiry
whether there should be one in the future. Men
say, "Oh, the Scottish Voluntaries may be thrown
out of account, for whatever rights they may
have, they will never claim them." It is a poor
and mean-spirited fallacy. They will claim no
rights as against the nation and people of Scotland—no, nor will you. I believe neither of you
have any such rights against the nation. Yet
you have rights under the nation, and so have
they ; and both you and they will claim them for
the nation and for yourselves as against any minority of the nation which withstands its rights and
yours. And no man need attempt to deceive or
to confuse you on such a subject as this. What !
you, the sons of the men of 1843, find a difficulty
in reconciling the ideas of right and relinquish-
ment, claim and self-sacrifice ! Why, what are
rights given us for in this world except to relin-
quish them for the good of others? Why were
the strong made, if not to serve the weak ? And
why do we draw breath on Scottish soil, if not, for
poor old Scotland's sake, first, to assert our rights,
and then to surrender them *to her* ?

For, Gentlemen, with all this talk of the rights
of Churches to endowments, let us remember that,
in the most important sense, these belong to
Scotland alone. And here again I am not using
metaphor or rhetoric. In the great war which
raged between the jurists as well as the theologians of Europe after the Reformation, three
points, I think, came to be thoroughly established,
as to the sense in which Protestant Churches
claim such things as State endowments—three
points in which their views differ from the
Romish views. In the first place, none of our
Churches claims temporalities as its own in the
absolute sense in which the Church of Rome has
for centuries done. And your Church in particular has acknowledged this most frankly—
acknowledged it in the very front of the Claim by
its General Assembly in 1842. Some things it
there claims absolutely and inalienably, as against
the State and every one else, but these are its
spiritual liberties. All Church temporalities, on
the other hand, it acknowledges, appertain to the
State, to do with them what it thinks just. No
doubt at that point your just claim comes in, but
still it is a claim the justice of which you will
present to the State, and then leave it to its disposal, as being of right the party to deal with it.

I acknowledge, indeed, that you are, even in this matter, in a very different position from that of the Established Church. You sometimes hear members of that Church speaking as if it had an independent right to temporalities which the State is bound to acknowledge. Now, that is using Free Church language by mistake. It is only a Church that is independent that can make a claim as being independent; and the decisions of 1843 have, I am afraid, a conclusive bearing on that matter. But even you, who preserved your independence at such a price, and protested that you should therefore at all times have right to come back to the Legislature, even you will come to the State on this matter, as being the party which is the judge and the authority—which in that capacity may, no doubt, do right or do wrong, but which in any case is the party to deal with it. And, secondly, when you ask the State to do justice, it does not follow that it is to do justice in the old form by simply restoring the endowments to you. I have already said enough on one branch of this, as to the equality of the rights of the other independent branches of the Church. I add now, that the State, on your principles, which are the common principles of Protestantism, if it deprives the Established Church of its present

exclusive and odiously unjust possession cf the
endowments, is bound, in distributing and using
them, to keep in view the whole Church of Christ
in the land, and, in particular, to consider its
constituency equally with yours. You do not
unchurch other Churches whose relations with the
State you consider unfortunate. And, while I
cannot recall what I have, in a separate form,
upheld, that the " Scotch Law of Establishment "
is, since 1843, a law of subjection in Church
matters to Parliament, I repeat now, what I have
taken every opportunity of maintaining, that,
whatever its leaders may do, the members of that
Church for themselves reject and refuse that
existing law, and would join you to-morrow if it
were put seriously into practice. There is absolutely nothing, except separation from the State,
that is needed to put the Established Church of
Scotland on the same footing of freedom and independence which you possess ; and there is nothing
in your principles, or in any others, to suggest
that the State, in dealing with the liberated
endowments, should not, as a matter of course,
deal with that Church, as, on a narrower proposal, one of the branches of the Presbyterian
Church, or as, on a larger, one of the branches of
the Church of Christ in Scotland. But, thirdly,

there is another point in your Protestantism
which has, perhaps, still more important bearings
on the matter of endowment. When these funds
come back for the disposal of the State, as the
party having proper right to deal with them,
neither it nor you are bound to apply them—
Church funds though they have been—to Church
purposes. In a Presbyterian Church there is no
such thing as sacrilege in the wise disposal of
funds and property. If you think that a secular
disposal of funds to which you have a right, or in
which you have an interest, is better—better for
the Church and better for the State—than
devoting it to its prior religious purpose, then you
are not merely entitled, you are bound in conscience, to secularise them ; and any Presbyterian
who thinks otherwise is not only a little of a
heretic, but a good deal of a fool. You do not
think so. You belong to the Church of him who
melted the silver apostles and sent them about
doing good; or rather—I say it reverently—you
belong to the Church of Him who said, "I have
called you not servants, but friends," and who
retains the power to make intelligible to each
generation of His servants His will for their work
and their day.

Now, I hold that these three considerations,

taken together, amount to this—that you and
Scotland stand in this matter in the same line;
that there is no inconsistency either between your
interests and that of your Presbyterian brethren,
or between your interests and that of your
nation; and that the more promptly and the
more strenuously you press your own rights, and
press them together, the better it is for our
common country, and for all parts and sections
of it. I need not say that in pressing the joint
rights of the disestablished Presbyterians, there is
a fitness in partitioning the different aspects of
what I hold to be essentially one claim. To the
United Presbyterians it belongs rather to press
your claim along with their own, as those of
citizens and members of the State. To you there
falls appropriately the honour and the duty of
urging their rights along with your own, as
together representing the ancient Kirk of Scotland, disinherited but free. You will more fit-
tingly press the common Presbyterian right to the
endowments—they, the duty of surrendering them
to Scotland; but your principles bind you to
surrender them to Scotland as certainly as theirs,
and their historical rights to every penny of the
endowments are as certain and as sacred as yours.

And do not think, Gentlemen, that I am

making either too much or too little of this
matter of demanding the endowments for Scotland. I know that your Claim of Right is funda-
mentally a claim for far other things—things
which do not depend on the will of any nation or
any civil power. And I know, too, that you have
learned to look with devotion and loyalty on a
Church apart from all idea of garniture and
endowments. You learned that on the day when
you had to make your choice, and when, as the
dear disinherited Church of Scotland passed into
the wilderness, you exclaimed in words as loyal
and as passionate as those of our native poet,—

> " I wadna gie her in her sark
> For thee wi' a' thy hunder mark ! "

But you hold that the hundred marks also belong
of right to her—the penniless lass with the long
ecclesiastical pedigree : and I agree with you, provided that you include all her features, and trace
her genealogy aright, and that you remember
that those who now seem to be opposed to you are
in blood and faith your friends. Only remember
also that the strength of your claim even to those
civil rights grows and accumulates with the
breadth of the basis on which you place them.
As the Free Church of Scotland alone you have a

claim conclusive against the present Church established, even if no other element came into account. As the same Church, forming part of, and, along with your ecclesiastical allies, representing the ancient and Free Kirk of Scotland, you have an impregnable historical claim to present even to the State. But when you blend these claims together and merge them in the rights—I do not say of the State, but of the people, of Scotland as a whole—you seem to me to occupy the surest and the strongest position, which includes all the others, and is mightier than them all.

THE THEORY OF THE CHURCH AND ITS CREED.

THE THEORY OF THE CHURCH AND ITS CREED,

WITH REFERENCE TO THE LAW OF SCOTLAND.

THE legal relation of a Church to its creed depends more or less on the true relation of a Church to its creed. Law, in the case of a Church tolerated, and still more in the case of an Established Church, may limit, enlarge, or modify this original idea, but it cannot dispense with it.

I. But what the true and original relation of a Church to its creed is, depends upon our theory of the Church. If we take one of the two great theories which have divided the world, it will lead us to different results as to creed from what we should have arrived at upon the other. The Church of Rome, the grandest and most powerful of human institutions, has always held one idea of the Church, an idea which in the nineteenth century has rapidly spread even among those who reject her claim to be its exclusive embodiment. According to this theory the Church is an external institute — a great visible corporation. It does not consist of the good alone, or of the regenerate, or of those who truly believe; for these are distinctions which only God can observe, and the Church must be before all things visible.[1] It consists of all, good and bad, who, even in hypocrisy or ignorance, *profess* Christianity, and join themselves to the external institute.[2] For this external institute is the divinely appointed medium of salvation, and age after age dispenses blessing and distributes truth to those who have been received into its fold.

The sixteenth century brought to the human

---

[1] "Nam cum illi ab omnibus parendum sit, cognoscatur necesse est."—*Catechism of the Council of Trent*, ch. x., sec. 11.

[2] "Hoc interest inter sententiam nostram, et alias omnes, quod omnes aliæ requirunt internas virtutes ad constituendum aliquem in ecclesia, et propterea ecclesiam veram invisibilem faciunt; nos autem et credimus in ecclesia inveniri omnes virtutes, fidem, spem, caritatem, et ceteras; tamen ut aliquis aliquo modo dici possit pars veræ ecclesiæ, non putamus requiri ullam internam virtutem, sed tantum externam professionem fidei, et sacramentorum communionem quæ sensu ipso percipitur."—BELLARMINE, *De Ecclesia Militante*, ch. ii.

race a passion for individual freedom and for individual access to God; and the immediate result was the formation of the theory of *the invisible Church.* The thoughts of men in one country after another of Northern Europe, at first perturbed by their new riches, soon clarified into theologies, and crystallised into creeds; and as we go from one of these "Confessions"[1] to another, we find that the new idea of the Church everywhere supplants the old. The process is easily understood. One-half of the maxim of Irenæus had been familiar to men for many centuries, "Ubi ecclesia, ibi Spiritus;" but the other was now, for the first time (since Pentecost and Paul), felt and accepted, "Ubi Spiritus, ibi ecclesia." And the result was an idea even more august than that which had so long fascinated the world and may charm it once more—an idea nowhere more adequately expressed than in our own Scottish Confession : "As we believe in one God, Father, Son, and Holy Ghost, so we most

[1] The Westminster Confession is declared by our chief statute to contain the sum and substance of the doctrine of the Reformed Churches. Nor is this the only expression which refers us to that doctrine. What it authentically is, is fortunately not difficult to find. We must seek it in the Confessions of and subsequent to the Reformation.

15

constantly believe that from the beginning there
hath been, and now is, and to the end of the
world shall be, one Kirk—that is to say, one
company and multitude of men chosen of God,
who rightly worship and embrace Him by true
faith in Christ Jesus—a Kirk invisible, known
only to God, who alone knoweth whom He hath
chosen."

Thus, according to the Romish idea, the Church
is an external institute for bringing men personally
to God; according to the Protestant idea, it is the
society of those who have come to God personally
already. In the one case, men join the Church
in order through its discipline to become true
Christians; in the latter, being true Christians
individually, they collectively form the Church.[1]
We need not pursue the Romish doctrine further;
but it will be of importance to understand how
this primary Protestant idea of the invisible

[1] In addition to Cardinal Bellarmine, the most authoritative theologian of Rome, we may quote her celebrated
modern defender, Moehler: "The differences between
the Catholic and the Lutheran view of the Church can be
reduced to a short, accurate, and definite expression. The
Catholics teach that the visible Church is first; then
comes the invisible : the former gives birth to the latter.
On the other hand, the Lutherans say the reverse : from
the invisible emerges the visible Church, and the former is

Church is connected with the secondary doctrine, which we also find in their Confessions, of the *visible* Church, and at what points in the transition from the one to the other there emerges the necessity for a creed. For all the Protestant Confessions, no less than the doctrines of Rome, acknowledge that the Church in some sense becomes invisible; that it is the duty of Christian men to recognise each other, and associate as such; and that communities so formed, though partial, and therefore not identical with the Church universal and invisible, and though mixed and impure, and therefore not coinciding exactly even with any part of it, are yet entitled to the name of Church, and, generally, are bound by the Church's laws, and may claim the Church's rights. But throughout them all it is plain that the invisible Church is the radical and original idea, the archetype upon which the external Church is framed. Indeed, so strong at first was the

the groundwork of the latter. In this apparently very unimportant opposition a prodigious difference is avowed." —*Symbolik*, ch. xlviii. "The Calvinists adopted Luther's general views respecting the Church without alteration, and solemnly confirmed them in their symbolical writings."—Ch. li. On this distinction, viewed from the Protestant side, an able treatise, *The Church of Christ*, by the Rev. E. A. Litton, was published in 1851.

revulsion from the Romish doctrine, that some of
the Confessions avoid any recognition of *one*
universal *Church visible,* acknowledging instead
particular Churches or congregations which are
visible. This comes out especially in that of
Scotland of 1560, where the chapter as to the
universal Church known only to God is followed
by the marks of particular Churches, "such as
were in Corinthus and Galatia," and such as we
" profess ourselves to have in our cities, towns,
and places reformed." A clause, indeed, towards
the beginning of this chapter seems to speak of
the "notes of *the* true Kirk;" yet there is no
attempt to treat of this as of a universal Church
visible, more fully or more definitely.[1] The
Church visible is treated as congregational or
aggregational. The unit is the individual, who
by his invisible faith is already really united to
God and to all other men who have faith, in a
universal invisible society; but he can only externally unite with those who are known and
accessible to him, and who also seem to his
fallible judgment to have the like gift which has
been given to himself. And thus we have one

---

[1] Moehler remarks the extreme Protestantism of the
Scottish Confession on the doctrine of the Church.—
Symbolik, ch. li. note.

invisible Kirk, and particular Kirks visible.
This course is not followed in most of the
other Confessions, which rather treat of the
invisible Church as in some way becoming visible,
without any attempt accurately to define the two.[1]
For the completed distinction and for a full recognition of a universal Church *visible*, we in this
country have to come down a century later to the
second standard of Scotland, which on this point
exceeds the mass of Reformed Confessions as much
as its predecessor fell short of them. The Westminster Confession of Faith, like the others, puts
the belief in the true Church invisible foremost.
But it goes on immediately to confess a visible
Church, Catholic and universal, of which particular Churches are members (reasoning thus,

---

[1] The following are two very good examples :—

" Ecclesiam, sanctam sanctorum omnium collectionem,
et immaculatam Christi sponsam, esse tenemus. Quæ
quidem quum *solius sit Dei oculis nota*, externis tamen
quibusdam ritibus, ab ipso Christo institutis, et verbi Dei
velut publica legitimaque disciplina, non solum cernitur
cognosciturque, sed ita constituitur, ut in hanc sine his
nemo (nisi singulari Dei privilegio) censeatur."—*Helretica
Prior Confessio* ch. xv. Niemeyer, 118.

" Ecclesia, quanquam id, unde habet quod vere Ecclesia
Christi sit (nempe fides in Christum), videri nequeat, ipsa
videri tamen, planeque ex fructibus cognosci potest."—
Confessio Tetrapolitana, ch. xv. Niemeyer, 758.

not from the parts to the whole, but from the
whole to the parts). This visible Church hath
been sometimes more, sometimes less, visible,
according to the purity of doctrine and discipline
which has existed; but it "consists of all those
throughout the world that profess the true religion and their children, and is the kingdom of the
Lord Jesus Christ, the house and family of God,"
and to it (not to the invisible Church) Christ hath
given the ministry, oracles, and ordinances of
God.[1]

This advance by the Westminster Confession
from the position occupied by those of the Reformation might suggest some interesting questions,
which must here be waived. But it is necessary
to remark that, with all this careful assertion of
the place and privilege of the one visible Church,
this Confession is deficient in a matter regarding
its visibility on which the former creeds are very
full and express—*i.e.*, the *notes* or marks of the
Church. These notes and marks are seemingly of
the *visible* Church or Churches, an invisible Church
admitting of none; and the Reformation Confessions are very careful, and, on the whole, very
harmonious in giving these tests. In the one
which is most interesting to us the Scottish Re-

[1] Westminster Confession, ch. xxv. See pages 93, 94.

formers give the essentials of a Church as, first, the true preaching of the Word; second, the right administration of the sacraments; and, third, ecclesiastical discipline uprightly administered. The difference between it and the majority of the Reformed creeds is that, while they all hold the third requisite—the exercise of ecclesiastical discipline—to be binding on a Church, most of them do not hold it to be so essential that the absence of it unchurches the body (as it has been expressed, it is not in the same degree of necessity); and therefore they do not make it a separate note.

II. If these observations, which the writer has gleaned with much self-distrust from an unaccustomed field, are correct, we should now be in a better position to judge what is meant when the Scottish lawyer is asked to deal with "a Church," or "the Church," or "the Church of Christ," and what the essential relation of such a body is to its creed.

It does not appear that, according to the Confessions of the Reformation, we can hold that the Church proper is *founded on doctrine* or truth. It seems rather to be therein founded upon the personal and vital relation of the individual to

God through Christ. It is certainly not founded,
as all agree, on any particular creed or expressed
Confession or formula of doctrine; but neither,
according to these authorities, does it appear correct to say that it is founded even upon truth, or
that its authority is derived from truth. Properly,
its authority is derived from Christ, and it is·
founded upon Christ. And yet the Church, though
not founded upon truth, may be definable and
recognisable only by truth. Its connection with
God and Christ may *make* the Church, and yet its
connection with truth may mark and express it.
For, according to the Reformed doctrine, this
fundamental and causal relation of the Church to
its Author is so far from being independent of
truth or of doctrine, that the Church has a constant and necessary relation to both. The Scottish
Confessions say that the grace of faith is that
"whereby the elect" (*i.e.*, the Church invisible)
"are enabled to believe to the saving of their
souls;" and "by this faith a Christian believeth
to be true whatsoever is revealed in the Word, for
the authority of God Himself speaking therein,"
the principal acts of saving faith being those
terminating upon Christ. If it be contended that,
even so, it is the subjective nature of faith that is
meant to be the tie between God and the indivi-

dual, and not the amount of objective truths
which happen to have been revealed to it, still it
is plain that these objective truths are the proper
food of this faith, and are all meant, sooner or
later, to be absorbed by it.   It may be that in the
Church invisible are (exceptionally) those who
know little or nothing of truth revealed, and who
are members of it by means of the vital grace
binding them to the Author of life; but the perfect and completed idea of the Church, even of the
Church invisible and individual, seems to be a body
living by faith upon God's revelation, and upon
Christ the centre of it.

While, therefore, it may be too strong to say
that the Church, even the visible Church, is
founded on truth or doctrine or creed, it is not too
strong to say that, according to the Confessions of
the Reformation, there is a necessary connection
between the Church and doctrine, and an almost
absolute necessity (including, of course, a liberty)
for the Church to set up a creed.   Indeed, in the
latest of these Confessions, which our law declares
to be the sum and substance of the others, the
visible Church is *defined* as "those who profess the
true religion."   Profession of the truth which he
has received is by all of them made necessary to
the character of every Christian man; and mutual

profession or confession of the truth, to some extent at least, is necessary to that mutual recognition which makes a Church visible. Before God,
faith; before men, confession, seems the true
order; and it is easy to see how, when we come to
speak of the recognition of a Church by others,
and especially by the law, it should appear (as in
Scottish history it does) to be founded on truth
rather than on life. For doctrine and the utterance of doctrine, truth and the confession of truth,
are essential to a visible Church—are part of its
visibility.

III. How far that confession may lawfully go,
how far it must necessarily go, and how far it
ought to go, are much more difficult questions.
The Reformation Confessions have marked their
idea of it by the full but not minute way in which
they travel over the doctrines involved in that
"preaching of the Word," which they make the
leading note of a Church. The Westminster Confession, by its still greater exactness, minuteness,
and consolidation, has left to us the view of that
time as to what those who "profess the true religion" ought to profess. Why, in either case,
they give so much, and why they do not go on to
give more, is nowhere authoritatively stated. It

is plain that it was not their endeavour to ascertain the absolute minimum of confession. On the abstract principles of Protestantism it might seem that mere profession of the name of Christ,[1] as made in baptism, with a promise "to observe all things whatsoever He hath commanded His disciples," might be confession enough to found a visible Church. But all of these documents imply the right of the Church not only to utter, but to demand of its members, more than this. Its right to utter more is plain. The whole of truth, according to their view, is the inheritance and property of the Church—*i.e.*, the Church invisible. It is called to cherish, not a part, but the whole, and, if need be, to confess it. And the members of the Church visible must confess so much at least as to satisfy each other that they "profess the true religion" (according to the Westminster Confession), or, according to the older Confessions, that they do not deny the Evangel.

But when we have got so far as to find that by the doctrine of the Reformed Churches a certain confession of truth is appropriate and necessary, the question how much it ought to include seems to be regulated by the purposes for which it is

---

[1] " Qui Christo nomen dederunt."—*Zwinglii Fidei Ratio*, ch. vi.

issued—a matter on which we do not find these
Confessions making distinctions.   A Confession
may be a mere utterance or manifesto emitted at
a particular time, but of no value after the occasion has passed away.   Or it may be an utterance
of a Church at a particular time, which ever after
retains an historical value, though no attempt is
made to make it a standard, or test, or even a
permanent Confession.   Or it may be a permanent
utterance or *declaratio* by the Church of its belief,
valuable to this effect so long as it is not recalled,
but not at all made use of as an internal standard
to which the views of members are to be conformed,
or as a test either of membership or office—a confession, not a standard.[1]   Or it may be both a
confession and a standard, a dogmatic rule according to which the Church judges all views of sacred

[1] This is the view of the two thousand Congregational
Churches of Britain ; but we find the distinction skilfully
put in an older source.

The preface written by Episcopius to the Confession of
the Remonstrants—*Declaratio Remonstrantium*—is interesting on one account at least.   His party were strongly
opposed to creeds, and had suffered much from that constructed by the Synod of Dort.   But a time came when
they found it necessary to have one themselves ; and to
Episcopius was intrusted the delicate task of vindicating
the use of creeds on behalf of those who had loudly de-
claimed against them.

truth, and up to the level of which it trains its people and invites its ministers; and yet it may not be made an antecedent test for either the one or the other.[1] Again, the subordinate standard may be made to serve the purpose of a test, by an ordinance that those who do not believe in it shall not be admitted to a certain privilege, or to a certain office, or even shall be no members of the Church society at all. And, lastly, this may be enforced, either in the case of ministers or members, by a demand for evidence of this belief, or at least for evidence of this profession of belief, as, for instance, by subscription.

The Church of Scotland has, as we have seen,

[1] This appears to be the view of Bishop Burnet in the well-known conclusion of the *History of His Own Times* :—

"The requiring subscriptions to the Thirty-Nine Articles is a great imposition : I believe them all myself; but as those about original sin and predestination might be expressed more unexceptionally, so I think it is a better way to let such things continue to be still the standard of doctrine, with some few corrections, and to censure those who teach any contrary tenets, than to oblige all that serve in the Church to subscribe them : the greater part subscribe without ever examining them ; and others do it because they must do it, though they can hardly satisfy their consciences about some things in them. Churches and societies are much better secured by laws than by subscriptions ; it is a more reasonable as well as a more easy form of government."

used in its history all these lines of circumvalla-
tion; and used them with the intention of being
stronger thereby. Whether they have always
been kept duly separate, whether the different
purposes of a creed have been justly distinguished,
and in particular, whether what is necessary for
the being and what is necessary for the well-being
of a Church have been discriminated, deserves the
consideration of theologians, because it may call
for the adjudication of lawyers. Rules which are
passed by a Church in the exercise of its legislative
power for its own higher well-being, may be altered
by the power that made them, in the same manner
as the by-laws of any other society. But Confessions which are the expression of the essential
principles of a Church, occupy quite a different
position. Yet the question demands the attention
of theologians on far higher grounds than that of
possible civil consequences. And of all Churches
in the world, those of Scotland are most bound
earnestly to consider such questions upon their own
merits. Roman Catholics and High Churchmen
assume a power in the Church to act on its view
of what is expedient in imposing dogmatic truth,
and their creeds need no other foundation. But
the Scottish Church never claimed such autonomy,
and it is against its principles. Sincerely or

insincerely, it has always disclaimed any right to command, and put forward its obligation to obey; and standing on this more sacred ground, it has never hesitated to utter the holiest words in the face of all earthly authority, and to warn men against interfering with a body regulated only by the will of God. But a Church which claims to be regulated by principle, not expediency—by the will of God, not by the wisdom of men—even in matters of detail, cannot honestly shrink from considering first principles on so important a matter as the use which it makes of its creed. It does not appear that this question has ever been carefully or deliberately considered, much less authoritatively decided, in the past history of Scotland. In the days of the Covenants the Church made individual adherence to the Confession of Faith obligatory on every one of its members, and indeed on every one of the lieges.[1] It had presented that Confession originally as "only necessary to be believed," and it had some years after accepted establishment from the State, on the footing that all its members held that Confession. So far it might seem that the creed of the Church of Scot-

---

[1] The "Martyr Renwick," in Ordination Services still extant, took his elders bound to "all the lawful acts of all the lawful General Assemblies of the Kirk of Scotland."

land was not only a confession of its fáith, not
only an internal standard of its doctrine, not only
a test for its teachers and office-bearers,[1] but a
far more important matter, *a test of membership*.
But in this matter of membership eminently the
Church professes to be regulated by the will of
Christ, receiving only those whom He has received, and rejecting only those whom He has
rejected—receiving all Christians, and rejecting
only those whom it judges not to be so. Only by
observing, or professing to observe, this rule, can
it be the Church—*i.e.*, the Christian community.
If it takes any other rule, it becomes a different
society, perhaps larger than the Church, or perhaps smaller, but in either case a human and
voluntary society, aiming at the highest and most
beneficent objects, but doing so upon a principle of
association which it has devised for itself.

IV. A creed which is to be a test of membership must necessarily, as we have seen, be a very
limited one, and that for the highest reasons.

[1] There is a legal difficulty in changing a Confession ; but
it is a much simpler matter to deal with the adherences re
quired from office-bearers. It seems to be quite in a Church's
own power. And ministerial intercommunion to the fullest
extent might take place between two Churches without
incorporation, provided union is desired.

But every Confession, even a mere Church manifesto, must necessarily be limited, and that on
obvious grounds of common sense. It is sometimes said to be the right, or even the duty, of the
Church to hold all truth—a position which can
only do harm by its ambiguity. It is certainly
not always the duty of the Church to confess all
truth. For whatever individuals severally may
do, the Church, with its one Confession, cannot
effect this. Thus, taking it for granted that all
the ministers of the Presbyterian Churches hold
ex animo all the propositions which the Confession
of Faith draws from Scripture, it is at least
certain that each of these ministers (who has
thought of these propositions at all) differs from
every other in the meaning, emphasis, order, and
relation in which he holds them; and further,
that he differs from every one else in some of the
ten thousand minor propositions which are outside
the Confession. There is no honest and sane man
who will pretend that any proposition in religious
truth constructed by others exactly expresses his
own view of that religious truth; and though it
may be constructed with sufficient care and com-
prehensiveness to *include* the views of a great
number of consentients, it is morally certain that
every one of these consentients differ from every

16

other, and from the objective proposition itself, in
the exact sense in which he understands it.[1]   Confessions are limited, therefore, even when we look
to what is attempted to be expressed in them.
But this is clearer when we look to what is necessarily left out. The Westminster Confession is
large enough; but for every one scriptural proposition there fixed, there are ten left unfixed—
the larger the circle of truth ascertained, the
larger is the circumference towards the unascer-
tained outside.   No Creed includes everything.
For there are no two men who agree in the interpretation of every detail of Scripture, except those
who decline to apply their minds to Scripture at
all.   These truisms are not yet useless in Scotland ;
and the recollection of them has at least a tendency
to remind us that the Church, in drawing the line
which *must* be drawn between the truth she con-
fesses and the truths she does not confess, has a
difficult work to discharge, and has need of some
principle—or at least of some guidance.

The *principle* that most readily occurs is that of
fundamentals and non-fundamentals, essentials

---

[1] Hence the natural scruple to sign the Formula that
this Confession is " the confession of my faith." Properly
speaking, the Confession is not the confession of the faith
of any one who signs it, but of all. None of them exactly

and circumstantials—*i.e.*, conforming the creed used for purposes of confession, to what must (expressly or implicitly) be used for purposes of membership. A distinction founded on this principle would have the advantage of being unsectarian and catholic, proper to the Church of Christ, simple and reasonable, and seemingly unchangeable and permanent. But it has great disadvantages. One is, that in the past it has been almost impossible to attain, at least wise men have despaired of finding it in any definite or useful form. Another is, that the weight of authority has been against even the seeking of it. In the history of Scotland, and in the Reformed Churches generally, it does not appear that the men who sought for the minimum of truth to confess, were the men who had most of the diviner spirit of truth. The greatest men and the best men (with some exceptions, like Baxter) seem hitherto to have been in favour of full creeds. Churchmen of capacity and earnestness—the men in whose heart the question, *How is* THE KING's *government to be carried on ?* continually burned—

agrees with it, but none of them contradicts it. In an important sense all Confessions are negative rather than positive—articles of peace rather than utterances of personal faith,

have felt their practical need of creeds for keeping
the Church together, and have agreed that they
are essential, if not to the being (*esse*), at least to
the well-being (*bene esse*) of the Church.[1]   And, on
the other hand, the men of tenderness of conscience,
and pure heart towards God and men, have leaned
not only to the confession of the permanently
central truth, but to the eager and solemn confession of whatever truth the time and its trial
called for—to its confession not only individually,
but by the unanimous or accordant voice of the
witnessing Church of Christ.

And this suggests another possible principle, or
another variation of the same principle; for if the
Church is not to confess all truth, nor only essential truth, it may perhaps properly have to confess
the *truth for the time*—*i.e.*, essential or central
truth *plus* the truth for the particular time.   If
the Church has already a creed in which it has
attempted to embody the central truth, it is
obvious that some separate manifesto is the proper
medium for uttering the more transitory applica-
tions of it; but there seems, on principle, no
serious objection to both being included in the one

---

[1] A Church without creeds is a barrel without hoops.
But was not the Church kept together originally by a
power from within?

larger Confession—always provided that that Confession is held open to continual revision, and is actually and in point of fact revised, as soon as the necessity for the addition to it has passed away.

But a different doctrine from this has had great influence in Scotland. A very prevalent, if not the most prevalent idea there, has been that the Church is not only entitled to add to her fundamentals of Christianity any truth the confession of which seems to her called for at the time, but that having done so, she must ever after retain it in her Confession as an *attainment* which she is never to resile from. The creed thus comes to be an historical accumulation or incrustation, many articles in which are binding upon the existing generation solely because they are true, and were appropriately or necessarily confessed by a generation before. Nothing can show the passion of the Scottish Church for historical separatism and national continuity more than the favour which a theory so remote at first sight from all Protestant principle, and so liable to the most damaging *reductio ad absurdum*, has found in this country. The *absurdum* has not been wanting in the accumulating testimonies of two centuries; but the love of Church identity is too strong for all minor difficulties. It requires some crisis of Christian obligation to drive a Church back upon its native [1] and essential principles; and to embolden it, while not declining any duty of the time, to reduce its permanent Confession to that which the universal Church can share.

V. We have said already that there seem important legal reasons why the non-established Churches of Scotland should give attention to the question, what their essential creed (as distinguished from their many historical and actual utterances) is to be. With regard to the Established Church the case is peculiar. No longer standing on the ground of an independent compact with the State, and subjected in many parts of its religious work to the authority of statute, it yet is probably freer in its Church jurisdiction than any Established Church in Protestant Europe, and (as recent decisions in both countries have shown) has a distinct advantage in this respect of the great and powerful Church of England. But whatever steps it may take in the direction of modifying its creed, or of modifying the subscription to it, must be taken through Parliament [2]—

[1] An Apostolic Father says of the members of the Church Πᾶσα ξένη πατρίς ἐστιν αὐτῶν, καὶ πᾶσα πατρὶς ξένη.

[2] With reference to the older Scottish statutes on this

a region where the abstract considerations with
which we are here concerned have not so much
influence, and where the voice of the Church itself
on the question is a voice of persuasion rather
than of authority. (Yet it speaks with legitimate power there, as now essentially a national
Church—living for the nation and by it, and so
entitled to appeal to the nation for every change
that furthers its usefulness.)

   But with Churches which are free, and which
desire to be so in respect of creed, the legal question is an important if not pressing one. A Church
is only free to hold a creed when it is free to leave
it; and it is not free to leave what is essential to
its Church existence. The non-established Presbyterian Churches were till lately in the awkward
position of (popularly) representing all their Confessions as essential, and at the same time of

matter, one curious distinction must be kept in view which
does not attain in England. Our Scottish statutes are
liable to desuetude—*i.e.*, they are repealable, not indeed
by mere disuse, but by a contrary custom. Lord Stair
says, "Our statutes, or our Acts of Parliament, in this
are inferior to our ancient law, that they are liable to
desuetude, which never encroaches on the other. In
this we differ from the English, whose Statutes of parliament, of whatever antiquity, remain ever in force till they
be repealed."—*Institutes of the Law of Scotland*, b. i.,
title 1.

claiming a Church right to change them all.
That legal questions would arise sooner or later upon
such a state of matters was certain ; and the subject
may be more calmly and wisely discussed before
such collision than after it.   The question is perhaps
partly a mere question of words, in a race which
has a strong vein of paradox ; [1] but paradoxes in
Scotland, as in that other

> " Noble nation, where
> The idea of a knife cuts real flesh,"

have often drawn blood.   And it is probably also,
in some degree, an ultimately insoluble problem—
especially in the region as to fundamentals of a
Church and of individual belief.   But between
these extremes there seems to lie a certain substan-
tial and practical question, so practical that it is
not clear how any civil judge could refuse to take
it up, and so difficult that it is impossible to say
what, in certain cases, might be the result.

Yet the old Church Party in Scotland has never
been much influenced by considerations of civil
law and civil consequences; and for a pure decision on matters so central and sacred, this is
perhaps no disadvantage.   Besides, its essential
conservatism has long since led it to invert what

[1] " Gens ratione ferox, et mentem pasta chimæris."

seems to be the Protestant *onus probandi* as to creed,[1] and to hold practically that those who would move towards reducing a Church's creed to the essentials of the Church's faith, must prove their case, and show that this is a duty of the present age. To prove this may be impossible. But considerations like the following fairly raise the question :—

1. It is not a matter of option with a non-established Church whether it shall found on the essentials of Christianity or not. For it has no other sanction. An Established Church *has*—has a sanction which, by the common sense of mankind and our ancient principles of law is of high practical importance. A non-established Church has no power but conscience. It is only as representing the catholic Church of Christ that it can draw a single young man to its ministry, or a single member to its congregations. And it is only by doing so broadly and *obviously*, that it can continue to have any power. It must be an awkward thing for such a Church to have a Confession that does not represent the essential creed

---

[1] That is, theoretically, the *onus*. The perusal of the Confessions of the Reformed Churches does not give me the feeling that their framers or students would have been much influenced by such a theory.

of the Church of Christ—much more to have a
Confession that does not seriously pretend to represent that creed.

2. In former times the Church, as well as the
law, of Scotland, seem to have had no difficulty in
ignoring or denying the Christianity of those who
did not accept the full Confession of Faith—
Scottish or Westminster. All members of the
Church find it impossible to do so now. Not only
innumerable individuals, but whole communities
and sects outside it, are warmly recognised as
Christian. Probably no man will now assert that
the existing Confession supplies a criterion for
discriminating between one who is a Christian and
one who is not; and certainly no man believes it.
But this makes short work of what would otherwise be a very difficult question—turns it from a
matter of theology into a matter of common
honesty. The fact is acknowledged; only the
application remains. The application may, indeed,
be difficult; but the burden of proof against communion or union rests unceasingly on those who
keep apart from men already acknowledged to be
fellow-Christians.

These considerations run rather too exclusively
in one line; and as the legal facts which press

Churches in general lie in the same direction, it may be well to remind ourselves, in closing, that whatever may be the case with the Church, the individual is unchangeably bound to acknowledge all truth that he knows; that men are bound to seek truth together, and together to hold it; that through truth God saves men; that in their dealings with truth and His Church God tries men; and that the spirit of truth and love, or the want of it, which we show in legislating upon such a matter, or discussing it, lies open to One who with no postponed or uncertain judgment judges according to every man's work.

A QUARTER OF A CENTURY
OF THE DEVELOPMENT OF THE THEORY
OF CREED.

A QUARTER OF A CENTURY
OF THE DEVELOPMENT OF THE
THEORY OF CREED.

THE twenty-five years which have elapsed since the last essay was written have seen a great advance in the question dealt with. When a volume on *The Law of Creeds in Scotland* was published in 1867, the chief Churches there were all bound to the unrevised Confession of Westminster. For it Scotland, long before the Revolution of 1688, had been willing to forsake its original national Confession—that laid by John Knox on the table of the Parliament of 1560— and every minister and elder was now bound to the new Creed by subscription. The United Presbyterian Church indeed, which since the later or European Revolution has represented the voluntary Church theory, had qualified its subscription in more ways than one. It asked subscription to the Westminster Creed and catechism on the understanding that the Church " did not approve

255

of anything in these documents which teaches compulsory and intolerant principles in religion." The intolerant passages referred to are those which the American Presbyterians cut out in revising the same Confession in 1788, and they are now universally condemned. Even the Free Church, when it left the State in 1843, felt the pressure of them so far as to pass an act to disclaim "intolerant or persecuting principles." But it still maintained subscription to the un-changed Confession. And the form of subscription in it and in the Established Church alike was still the very strict one dating from 1711 : "I do sincerely own and believe the whole doctrine contained in the Confession to be the truths of God, and I do own the same as the confession of my faith." The United Presbyterians had already adopted a more reasonable formula, sub-scribing the Confession generally "as an exhibition of the sense in which I understand the Holy Scriptures."

But already the waters had been stirred. In 1866 the two General Assemblies, claiming to repre-sent the Church of Scotland historically, met as usual on the topmost ridge of Edinburgh. Each elected its moderator, and the moderator took for his subject the question of Creed. In the

Free Church Assembly its chairman, Dr. Wilson, took the lead by the statement that " no confession of faith can ever be regarded by the Church as a final and permanent document. She must always vindicate her right to revise, to purge, to add to it. We lie open always to the teaching of the Divine Spirit ; nay, we believe in the progressive advancement of the Church into a more perfect knowledge of the truth." Ten days later Dr. Cook, the Moderator of the Church of Scotland, closed his Assembly in the presence of the Queen's Commissioner by a statement that the Scottish Dissenting Churches were no doubt free to change or modify the creed. " But it is not so with the Established Church. Our Confession, submitted to the estates of Parliament, was accepted as the truth of God ; and the Church was endowed and established, not free at any time to modify, alter, or depart from it, nor to hold the truth of any of its doctrines an open question." This utterance, listened to at the moment with submission, became three days later the occasion of a weighty protest by some seventy ministers led by Principal Tulloch. They did not question the alleged constitutional position of the Church. But they urged that, as Dr. Tulloch had said in his pamphlet two years before, " the old relation of

17

our Church to the Confession cannot continue."
For even if, and all the more if, the Creed and
subscription remained unchanged, the administration of doctrine in such a Church should be most
liberal and tolerant.

On neither side, however, did the discussion so
initiated result in any actual change. The Free
Church was at the time negotiating for union
with the United Presbyterian Church; a body
whose general sympathies on doctrine were very
much akin to its own, while its position on Church
freedom and civil freedom was distinctly in advance.
But in the former body the expected unanimity
was wanting, and the two Churches, when in 1873
they postponed the question of incorporation, did
not even carry out that "co-operative union"
which the Free Church minority had offered to
promote. Nor for many years afterwards did
the latter body appear to proceed upon any plan,
good or even bad, at least in this region of its
work. In the Church established on the other
hand, the dissatisfaction with the confessional
doctrine took, during the next ten years, such an
active form as to merit the description of a kind
of "Religious Upheaval."[1] Yet its ablest representatives, such as the two Principals of St.

<hr>

[1] *Contemporary Review*, *XXX.*, 240,

Andrews, Dr. Tulloch and Dr. Cunningham, were not in favour either of revising or abolishing that document. And the movement was a domestic one, not affecting the other Presbyterian Churches, except on one remarkable occasion. Dean Stanley, in his four lectures delivered in Edinburgh in January 1872, urged upon all Scotland the advantage of acquiescing in an Erastian and essential connection of the Scottish Church with the State. That argument, powerfully put, was at least as powerfully met on the platform;[1] but the other question at the same time indirectly, but pervasively, raised—the expediency of subscription by men to a statutory Creed which they need not believe—created a situation of considerable danger. Of the apprehensions then felt, the paper which follows this may serve as a memorial, all the more as proposals substantially the same are sure in some form and at some time to recur. Fortunately Dean Stanley's skilful and kindly suggestions of 1872, like the Patronage Legislation of 1874, roused a widespread resistance and even reaction ; and this went so unreasonably far within the Church, as in 1877 to induce the General Assembly, under the Moderatorship of Dr. Phin,

---

[1] Principal Rainy's memorable reply is published as *Three Lectures on the Church of Scotland.*

to reject the proposal for a relaxation of the subscription by elders, afterwards in a cognate form carried out.

Ten years had thus slipped away unredeemed. But a new start was made in the most legitimate way by the meeting in Edinburgh in 1877 of the first Council of the Presbyterian world from both hemispheres. One of the earliest feelings aroused by that remarkable gathering was the sense of the diversity, variety, and multiplicity of administration which were to be found within the supposed rigidity of Presbyterianism. In some things this came to Scotsmen as a revelation, for twenty or thirty Creeds were already represented even in that first Council. And in nothing was it more important to bring out the combination of unity in the substance with variety in the detail, than in the matter of Creed. Accordingly, at the very first public sitting of the Council, the present writer proposed a committee which should gather together and tabulate all the Creeds and confessions of the fifty Churches from all parts of the world which were represented in the room, with the formulæ of subscription or other adherence demanded from church officials or members. The proposal, seconded by Principal Tulloch, was unanimously agreed to, but it took three years to carry it out. And the result (presented by Dr. Schaff to the Second or Philadelphia Council in 1880) was very interesting. It showed that this large Christian body, divided by the Atlantic into two not unequal parts, and now no longer connected with any particular state or nation, was still resting historically on the new Puritan Creed of 1647. But all the free churches had more or less revised their connection even with that new Creed: some, in America, only tied themselves to the "system of doctrine" contained in it; others, in Scotland, held it "an exhibition" of their understanding of Scripture; others, like the Welsh Calvinists in 1827, had exchanged it for a Creed wholly different in form, but alike in substance; and others, including almost all the smaller Protestant bodies scattered over Europe, had in this century adopted, instead of it, short utterances of central and saving truth. By this result the principle of Protestant freedom, from details and from documents, was fully vindicated; and the wise constitution by which the new ecumenical Assembly was made in the first instance a consultative body merely, with only a moral authority, left the churches included in it free to take each its own way in their common path.

In Scotland the United Presbyterian Church,

as had been expected, at once took the lead in legislation. The controversy in which, a generation earlier, the names of Dr. Balmer and Dr. John Brown had appeared, made it easier to contemplate the revision now for some years urged. It made it certain, too, that the revision, when it came, would include an assertion of the "general reference" of the Atonement and the Gospel to all mankind to whom it is offered, as well as its "particular reference" to those who actually embrace it. This great subject of the love of God in the Gospel accordingly became one centre of a supplementary or Declaratory Act passed by this Church in May 1879, the other being naturally furnished by the persecuting clauses of the Westminster Creed. The main body of the Presbyterian family, that across the Atlantic, had long ago deleted the clause by which not only the Church with its censures, but the "magistrate" by his "power," may proceed against men who merely publish opinions, provided only the opinions are contrary to the "known principles of Christianity," or even to "the external peace and order" of the Church, or even to "the power of godliness." This was of course also rejected here, and instead of the old duty of the State to support and to suppress religions, a positive obligation was affirmed,

as laid upon the Church by Christ, to maintain
her own ordinances by free-will offerings. And
generally, in addition to these points, (in which
Scripture teaching was merely alleged to be set
forth "more fully. and clearly" than in the old
standards,) the Act declared that "liberty of opinion
is allowed on such points in the standards, not
entering into the substance of the faith, as the
interpretation of the six days in the Mosaic account of the creation, the Church guarding against
the abuse of this liberty to the injury of its
unity and peace." All this " Declaratory Act " pro-
ceeds on a preamble that the standards, " being of
human composition, are necessarily imperfect," and
wound up with the provision that the formula,
acknowledging the confession and catechisms as
an exhibition of the sense in which Scripture is
understood, should have the words added, " this
acknowledgment being made in view of the explana-
tions contained in the Declaratory Act of Synod
thereanent."

While one Church was thus definitely but
cautiously advancing, another was struggling amid
much confusion with principles which necessitated
change. In the Free Church the questions emerged
on the side of scholarship, and naturally arose
first in its powerfully equipped colleges. Professor

Robertson Smith, a young but distinguished teacher, had become both Hebrew Professor of the Free Church and Editor of the new *Encyclopædia Britannica*. As early as 1876 some of his articles there had raised strong feeling, especially one in which Deuteronomy was represented as written, ages after Moses, in a dramatic form selected for his own purposes by the sacred author. The Free Church College Committee at once met, but found there was no ground for a process for heresy; and Mr. Smith's presbytery might have taken a similar course, but the professor, to the general surprise, rather challenged a prosecution under the Westminster Confession, which, he alleged, favoured his doctrine of Scripture. That doctrine he deliberately laid down in his answer to the Presbytery's "libel" or accusation. Scripture, he held, is only divine, and is only infallible, where it reveals to us "that knowledge of God and His will which is necessary to salvation." To that element, and to that alone, there is the witness of the Spirit. In other respects it is to be proved, where it can be proved, by the ordinary modes of historical evidence. This broadening of the question gave much more importance to the decision of the Assembly of 1880, which, in dismissing the only charge against its professor which was still urged, declared "that the Free Church, in declining to decide on these critical views by way of discipline, expresses no view in favour of their truth or probability, but leaves the ultimate decision to future inquiry in the spirit of patience, humility, and brotherly charity." The suggested truce, however, was broken before the year was out upon the appearance of other and stronger Encyclopædia articles previously sent to the press. The next Assembly still refused to try their professor, as he still demanded, by the old creed, but by a large majority summarily resolved, that it was no longer safe " or advantageous for the Church that Professor Smith should continue to teach." All through this controversy in Scotland there had been a feeling of perplexity and paradox. The young men and the innovators took their stand upon the old paths, and professed the highest regard for the existing standards. The old and the conservative declined to be bound by these documents, and made their appeal rather to popular and traditional feeling. In particular, the violent procedure of 1881 was manifestly prompted by indisposition to enter at once and publicly upon the field of prolonged "inquiry," which the Assembly had the year before invited ; for such an inquiry would have involved the question, not merely whether the critical views were within the existing Creed, but whether that Creed itself was adequate for the time and its crises. Not till three years had passed did the gradual and un- conscious advance of the Christian mind in this communion take effect in an enactment as to deacons. These office-bearers, comprising a great army of the younger men of the Free Church, had since 1843 signed the same doctrinal formula with teachers of doctrine. With all ministers and elders they were bound to the " whole doctrine " of the Westminster Confession. This absurd uniformity was now broken, and the deacon, called "to administer the temporal affairs of a congregation," was released from that document, and bound only to "own and receive, as in ac- cordance with Holy Scripture, the *system of evan- gelical truth* taught in this Church, and set forth in the Westminster *Shorter Catechism.*"

Three years more—the whole of a second decade—had passed before the question was raised for the unrelieved ministers and elders. It was raised in the two churches simultaneously about the year 1887; but the Established Church of Scotland was first to attain success, or such a share of success as could fairly be demanded, con-

sidering its relation to the State. The Assembly
of 1888 simplified the oral "Questions" to be
addressed to office-bearers, stripping them not only
of the rejection of "Bourignianism," which even
the Free Church since 1843 has counted unnecessary, but of a number of other negations. The
most important change, however, is the substitu-
tion for the interrogatory, "Do you believe the
Scriptures of the Old and New Testaments to be
the Word of God, and the only rule of faith
and manners?" of the following form, "Do
you believe the Word of God which is *contained*
in the Scriptures of the Old and New Testaments to be the supreme rule of faith and
morals?" In the other department of subscription, it had been proposed now, as some years
previously, to withdraw all subscription from the
creed of Westminster. But an influential Committee had been appointed to inquire into the
subject, and they reported to the Assembly that
the only practicable change in the matter of subscription was "to bring the practice of the Church
into accordance with statute law." Fortunately,
in the case of elders there is no statute, and this
enabled lay rulers to be allowed henceforth simply
to "subscribe their approbation" of the Confession.
Even this is a strong step for any of them who

should hold, as the Chairman of the Assembly Committee in proposing it to the Assembly stated he held himself, that the document to be approved "puts Calvinism in the most offensive possible way." But it is more serious to retain a clerical subscription which "sincerely owns" the doctrine (statute does not demand the "whole" doctrine) therein contained and thus described, and even declares the Confession or its doctrine to be "the confession of my faith." Yet in this statutory form it has been retained by the Assembly. No one doubts that the tendency of that body as a whole towards dogmatic breadth has of late years increased rather than diminished; and a preamble to the Act declares that ungrudging effect is to be given to tolerance in administration. But the new *animus* towards freedom of the administering Church does not change the old *animus imponentis* of the enacting State, and the statutory formula remains until Parliament is asked to break or vary the bond.

The Free Church had far less excuse for its delay in dealing with the same problem; but the movement in it, also, coming to the surface about 1887, gave promise at last of being something more than makeshift and provisional.[1] Principal

[1] See *The Theological Review*, Edinburgh, November 1888.

Rainy (who now held almost alone that leader-
ship of the Free Church which, after 1843, had
been divided among so many men of the highest
eminence) became Moderator in this year. " It
might be desirable," he had written fifteen years
previously, "to secure that, on any fair call, the
Church's attention should be directed to any part
of the Confession supposed to require revision, not
as a singular and revolutionary step, but as something belonging to her ordinary and recognised
responsibilities." The Moderator's powerful opening address, characteristically, neither encouraged
nor repressed the movement, but urged the Church
to consider that it was in " one of those times of
rapid and remarkable movement which are critical
in human history." Till the winter of 1888 there
was no action in the Presbyteries, but their overtures came to the table of the Assembly in the following May. The impulse to movement had been
originally derived from the pressure of subscription
to the "whole doctrines" of the Confession. For
among its minor doctrines some were notoriously
false, and others, even if true, notoriously unnecessary to be enforced on Christian office-
bearers ; and in both classes of cases the demand
for such a subscription, especially from young
men, was now felt to be shameful. But in the

Assembly more general considerations also found their place. Principal Brown, the venerable head of the Theological Hall of Aberdeen, in moving that while the Church must adhere to the great doctrines of its Confession, there was a present "call to deal with" its relation to that document, pointed out that the Westminster divines had not only put too many things into their creed, but had inverted their proper order. The theological centre of gravity, he had before said, was not now where the framers of that document had put it. Dr. Walter Smith, poet and preacher, held that the centre of gravity should be no longer the sovereignty of God, but the love of God; and Dr. Thomas Smith, while leading the inevitable protest against any change, yet confessed that, if he had to frame a theology, he certainly should not frame it even on the lines of the Confession. The motion for a committee was accordingly carried in this Assembly of 1889 by more than three to one; and as the great majority of the dissentients subsequently agreed to serve upon it, it became a very representative body—not unfit for that "ordinary necessary" work to which a Church, which has for two centuries neglected the duty of creed adjustment or revision, must for some time look forward. In the meantime, how-

ever, it has only succeeded in framing, with much
care, a Declaratory Act, very much on the lines
of those which the United Presbyterian and other
bodies have already accepted. It was passed by
the Assembly of 1891, and involves that question
of the adjustment of subscription formula, which
probably should have been the first taken up.
The largest matter, however, with which it may
have to deal was remitted to it by the same
Assembly, upon a resolution of the Presbyterian
Church in the United States, to "invite the co-
operation of the Reformed Churches throughout
the world, holding the Presbyterian system, to prepare a short Creed containing the essential articles
of the Westminster Confession, to be used as the
common Creed of these churches." This is proposed, not as a substitute for the creed of any
particular denomination, but to supplement these
documents for the common work of the Presbyterian Church, especially in mission fields. And
with this world-wide suggestion, our notice of the
development, for a quarter of a century,[1] of one
question in one province of the whole Christian
world may fitly close.

[1] A somewhat fuller treatment of the same period may
be found in the *Andover Review* (Boston), July 1889, and
Christian Leader (Glasgow), August 1889.

THE QUESTION IN SCOTLAND TWENTY YEARS AGO.

THE QUESTION IN SCOTLAND
TWENTY YEARS AGO.

D R. STANLEY went down to Edinburgh in
January last,[1] and gave four lectures on the
history of the Church of Scotland, which have
had, and are likely to have, a remarkable fortune.
The admirers of the Dean as a historian have
been disappointed with them. They say they are
not up to his mark. We may, I think, find reason
to believe that this is because they were not
intended by him to be properly historical essays.
Still, whatever be the reason, English readers have
again missed what they have often desired, and
what Dean Stanley could have executed for them
better than any man living or dead—a short,
complete, and luminously intelligible sketch by
the hand of genius, unfolding once and for ever
from within outwards that very tangled affair,
the ecclesiastical history of Scotland. This has
not been attempted, and has certainly not been

---

[1] _i.e._ 1872. See _Contemporary Review_ for March.

accomplished. No one will come to understand
Scottish Church History by reading the volume.
It unfolds nothing, either in order of time or of
principle. It is simply a picturesque pamphlet—
four turns of the historical kaleidoscope, with the
objects admirably selected and arranged for the
purposes of the exhibitor.

But if Dean Stanley has in this instance failed
in writing history, it is because he has been doing
a more important thing—making history. The
contents of his lectures are, according to Charles
Lamb's translation of *sermoni propiora*, "properer
for a sermon"; for while in them he has been
teaching Englishmen from the past history of
Scotland, he has been preaching to Scotchmen
what their future history should be. This view
has been universally accepted in the north, and
rightly. Dr. Stanley is too well known in Scotland
as an author for his central and significant
position as a Churchman not also to be understood ; and Edinburgh men who would have passed
a mere English bishop without curiosity went to
hear him with eager anticipation. They were
certain that, however others might content themselves with mere comments, edifying or amusing,
on the varied scenes of their history, it was a moral
impossibility for the Dean of Westminster to do

so. That most mild but at the same time cease-
less and consuming zeal which animates him could
scarcely be laid aside on such an occasion. In
voluntarily choosing the Kirk as his subject, he
had elected to deal with the very embodiment of
the two principles in opposition to which he has
for some time seemed to breathe—the passion for
doctrinal truth on the one hand, and church
independence on the other. The result of such
a collision would at any time have excited the
widest interest in Scotland, even if it had not
drawn forth in Professor Rainy a champion of
Presbyterianism, under whose intellectual prowess
smoulders an extraordinary moral power. The
Scottish Episcopalians, too, are much irritated at
being invited by an English dignitary to accept
an ancillary attitude towards a fragment of that
Presbytery which they once hoped to replace, and
equally so by his putting it on Erastian grounds.
But it appears to me that the thing which has,
on the whole, caused the greatest interest in these
utterances of Dean Stanley is the revelation of
a hitherto unacknowledged crisis in the Established Church of Scotland—a crisis which the
Dean's lectures have brought out so vividly to
the minds of Scotchmen that they have almost
seemed to create it,

For in Scotland the Dean of Westminster's
defence of Establishment has struck men with
the force of a paradox. They feel dimly that
Establishment, in the whole history and legislation
of those northern parts, has been not so much
different from the Broad Church idea as directly
opposed to it. In Scotland the Church has always
been supposed to be established for the sake of
the truth to which it was the witness. It was
indeed hardly too much to say that our Establishment was, originally, before all things the establishment of truth, and of doctrine which is the
form of truth. Statute after statute, Covenant
after Covenant, the Claim of Rights, the Revolution Settlement, the Treaty of Union, every transaction in which for hundreds of years the State
dealt with the Kirk, observes carefully the order
laid down by William III.'s Parliament, " in the
first place to settle and secure the true Protestant
religion as it hath of a long time been professed
within this land, *as also* the government of Christ's
Church within this nation." It need not be said
how contrary this, the popular idea in Scotland,
is to the conception of a National Church as held
by the school headed by Dr. Stanley—a school
dominant for the moment in English literature,
though provincial and insular if we take even

the modern world as a whole, not to speak of the
wider world of theology. The latter theory, with
its necessary surrender of the idea of establishment as being in any way a homage to truth, is
not only new and strange, but is abhorrent to the
Scotch mind. The essential obligation of a National
Church to conform itself and its creed to the nation
is one recognised by only a very small section of
Scottish Churchmen, and by them scarcely avowed.
It is a doctrine which circumstances have strongly
recommended to the more thoughtful minds, but
which the mass of the people still implacably
reject. And the skilful and cautious presentment
of it by its greatest teacher has had anything but
the effect of reconciling them to it.

No doubt, legally, Dean Stanley is right. On
the principles of the great judicial decisions of
1843, it is certain that, if Parliament were next
year to ordain the Church of Scotland to set up
the worship of the Virgin Mary, or to ignore in its
Confession the Divinity or Atonement of Christ,
it and all its ministers and elders would be bound
to do so. They would be bound, both legally and
morally, to do it—provided they continued members
of the Church. Individuals could save themselves
by seceding from it ; but since 1843 the Church
has no longer the right, under any provocation,

of separating from the State, any more than it
has, without separating, to disobey a controlling
statute.   Now, to Dr. Stanley this appears the
best and the only true relation between the State
and the Church, and we all know how very much
may be said for it.   There is, in the first place,
no danger that such enactments will be passed,
at least until the Scottish members of Parliament
and the majority of the people who elect them
demand it.   And if Scotland shall wish such a
change, why should the Church of Scotland refuse
it ?   Then in present circumstances it is clear that
any coming change will not be in the direction
of imposing doctrine or ritual on the unwilling
Church.   It will be rather in the direction of
sponging out doctrine and enlarging the freedom
of discipline and ritual : a change in which the
English Parliament, and especially the Scottish part
of the Legislature, would above all things study
to carry with them the majority of the Church.
And if the recently defined constitution of the
Church is not likely to entail any practical col-
lisions, why should not Dean Stanley maintain,
even in Edinburgh, what he has always consistently proclaimed elsewhere, that "the circum-
stance that all changes in the doctrine and ritual
of the Church must in the last resort be deter-

mined by the voice of the whole nation as expressed in Parliament," is to the Church itself
a "guarantee of justice, freedom, and enlighten-
ment"?[1] There was just one reason why he
should not. The people, not of the Free Church
and United Presbyterians merely, but the people
within the Established Church of Scotland, are
still dead against it. It is true that only half
the Church felt so outraged by the settlement
of principle in 1843 as to break with the State.
But abstract principle is one thing; carrying it
out is another. As he himself said, in a passage
which evoked a general growl in his otherwise
most courteous audience, "there is no other
country in the world where the consciences of so
many excellent people could have been wounded
to such a degree by the intricacies of a legal suit"
as to issue in the solemn farewell to Establishment of Dr. Chalmers and his fellows. But every
Scotchman knows that if the principles then
settled were now to be acted upon by the Legislature—I do not say in the way of intruding English
High Churchism or Broad Churchism on the
Kirk, but even in statutorily compelling the
most minute observance, however unobjectionable

[1] *Essays on Questions of Church and State.* 1870.
Preface, p. 27.

otherwise—another huge secession would instantly occur, and three-fourths of the laity of the Established Church would involuntarily adopt the language of the Church's independence which had been so familiar to their fathers.

But there were considerations which justified Dr. Stanley in making the attempt. There is in the Established Church of Scotland a small but influential section of Broad Churchmen, to whom circumstances have given a wholly disproportionate and for the present nearly dominant power. They are strong in the sub-consciousness that they, and they alone, hold views consistent with the legal position of their Church. And they are far stronger in the general sense of justice which urges an Established Church, especially one which seems to number only a minority of the population, to abandon religious and doctrinal distinctions which exclude others from national and even pecuniary privileges. And lastly, they are strong in that doctrinal Broad Churchism which most cultivated men profess; and while in some of them it is quite consistent with an honest attachment to the Creed, in others it takes the form of a persistent and corrosive opposition to it. As a consequence of all this, the steady and skilful effort to liberate the younger minds from the

statutory fetter of the Confession of Faith, and to
smooth out the more marked features of Scottish
Christianity, has been crowned with more success
than could have been expected. At present no
doubt the large majority of the Assembly honestly
love the hereditary faith of Scotland. But how
it may be ten or even five years after this is a
matter on which the odds are freely given and
taken in the Parliament House, or wherever
critics congregate. Already, even before Dean
Stanley came down, thinking men forecast the
time when broadening the Kirk according to his
view must be the only refuge from that disestablishment the shadow of which has for the last
three years haunted its conscience. It seemed
a great opportunity; and there was reasonable
ground to hope that the leading men of the
National Church, however strongly opposed privately to the sense in which the lecturer was to
advocate Establishment, would at least be willing
to say nothing, and not openly repudiate it.

Accordingly the Dean of Westminster came
down, and, in four lectures read before the Edinburgh Philosophical Institution, passed with swift
and graceful, but sometimes inaccurate, finger
over the whole history of Scotland, addressing now
Episcopalians, now Free Churchmen, and now

Voluntaries and Cameronians, but always looking forward to the conclusion best expressed in the following striking summing up [1] :—

" While insisting on the elements of Scottish religious life, which are above and beyond all institutions and parties, I should be shrinking from my task to-night if I did not ask what institution—I will not say what party—but what institution most corresponds to these aspirations ? And here I cannot doubt that, viewing it as a whole, and with all allowance for its short-comings, it must be that institution which alone bears on its front, without note or comment, the title of ' The Church of Scotland.' As of the Church of England so of the Church of Scotland, and so of every national church : its glory is, according to the golden maxim of the ever-memorable Hailes, to carry like the prophet a blank shield with no device of sect or party. . . Whatever Scottish Christianity is prepared to become, that the Church of Scotland ought to be prepared to be. It treats, or ought to treat, Pres-byterianism, Episcopacy, Patronage, Non-intrusion, as in themselves mere accidents. It has gone through the successive phases of the wild, monastic clanship of the Culdees, of the Anglo-Norman hierarchy of St. Margaret, of the Scottish hierarchy of Robert Bruce, the mixed Presbyterian and Episcopal government under Queen Mary and James VI., the mixed Epis-

[1] My quotations were from a newspaper report which seemed to have been taken from the manuscript : the volume had not been published.

copal and Presbyterian government under Charles I. and Charles II., and the purely Presbyterian government from William III. downwards. It has passed through the Liturgy and Confession of John Knox, through the Solemn League and Covenant, through the Sum and Substance of Saving Doctrine, the Westminster Confession and Westminster Directory ; and again, the alternations of domination from the Regent Moray to Andrew Melvil, to Rutherford and the Covenanters, to Carstairs and the Moderates, to Chalmers and the popular party. None of these phases need be—none ought to be—altogether lost to it. The Westminster Confession, no less than the Solemn League and Covenant, will always be treasured up among its historical documents, though both may have ceased to express the exact mind of the modern Church of Scotland. Its independence, its romance, its exquisite and unrivalled humour, its fervour, its prudence— these are the true heirlooms of the Church of Scotland, which it has never lost from first to last, and which, whatever be the change of its outward forms, it need never lose."

The proposal to the Church with the majestic Puritan creed to adopt a blank shield, and to hold Presbyterianism, and seemingly even Protestantism, as a mere phase in its history, and the recommendation to other Scotchmen to join it *because* of this proposed colourlessness, was bold for even Dean Stanley. But he spoke the carefully considered convictions of a lifetime, and no one

supposed that he had any other interest in the
matter than that of a student and statesman.
And the lectures, hasty and imperfect historically, were a marvel of conciliatory zeal, corus-
cated with the most contrasted sympathies, and
throughout recalled that mild light which glows
upon every page of Dr. Stanley's writing, which
shines but never burns, and leaves no scar upon
any human heart.

And yet they have missed their mark in Scotland, and I venture to think they ought to do so.

The minor inaccuracies are of little importance,
were it not that they are generally so manifestly
due to the haste to enforce the questionable
moral.[1] Thus the little sect of the Sandemanians
was contrasted with the great body of the Seceders, nothing being said of the famous " Marrow "
controversy of the latter, where the freeness of the
love of God in the Gospel was the point jealously
guarded by the Erskines against the orthodox
Moderates, while the Sandemanians are praised
for their " simple and unostentatious piety," and
Sandeman, their leading theologian, is singled out
as teaching in an " inoffensive attitude." The

---

[1] Some of the inaccuracies noticed in this and other
criticisms do not appear in the Lectures in their final and
published form.

fact is, that the theology of the Sandemanians
was a strong Hyper-Calvinism, the leading tenet
of which insisted on saving faith as a purely intellectual and unemotional act; and Sandeman in
particular, while a writer of the highest ability,
is perhaps the most keenly intolerant of all controversialists. The late Dr. John Duncan (whose
Colloquia[1] Dean Stanley justly praises, and who
had more liberality and learning, as well as more
mass of intellectual manhood generally, than any
professed Broad Churchmen who at present exist
in Scotland, or are likely to do so to the end of
the century) used to say, that Sandeman was the
only theological writer he knew comparable to
Swift for purity of style and bitterness of sentiment.[2] A still stronger instance of "premature
construction" is seen in Dr. Stanley's reference

[1] *Colloquia Peripatetica* (Edinburgh, 1870), from which
Dr. Stanley made several admirable quotations, but missed
the sentence bearing on his theme : "The best of our
fathers were more anti-Erastian than anti-Episcopal, and
more opposed to a bad liturgy than anti-liturgic."

[2] A saying of old Glas, Sandeman's father-in-law, himself
a good and pious man, though too weak to impress his
influence on his community (which has become the coldest
and most unemotional of all existing sects), was told
me by Dr. Duncan with intense appreciation. "Oor
Robert," old Glas used to say, speaking of Robert Sandeman—"Oor Robert first states the truth clearly, and then
he says, 'Gin ye dinna see it, Deil pyke oot yer een.'"

to Whitefield: " It was from the Church of the
Moderates, not from the Church of the Covenanters, nor yet of the Episcopalians, that three
thousand communicants went forth to receive
the Holy Eucharist from what Seceders called the
' foul, prelatic hands ' of the English clergyman " ;
and he adds that when the parish minister of
Cambuslang sent for him to assist him in that
great Revival, the Seceders denounced them both.
Now, if there is anything certain in the history of
the last century, it is that the Moderates were
unanimous in scoffing at Whitefield with the whole
energy of their shallow natures, and that the
" Church of the Moderates," exactly in proportion
as it was under Moderate influence, contemned
and denounced him, as they did the parish minister
of Cambuslang and all within their own borders
who shared in the great preacher's spirit. No
doubt the Secession quarrelled with him ; but why ?
Not because they were less willing to receive him
than M'Culloch of Cambuslang and the Evangeli-
cals, who belonged to their own school within the
Church but had not seceded ; but precisely for the
contrary reason—because they had first discerned
his greatness and invited him to Scotland, and so
unwisely claimed that he should preach for and
with them alone. And so he preached from

Evangelical pulpits inside the Establishment, to the indignation of the Moderate party, who had not at that time got their Act passed excluding such interlopers from pulpits—an Act which subsisted from 1799 till it was repealed by the Evangelical party, augmented by the return of not a few Seceders, in 1842. But these are mere straws that show the swiftness of the indiscriminating current in so candid a mind. They were adduced as tending to prove that in Scotland, as everywhere else, Establishment is a liberal thing and Dissent is both narrow and narrowing. Now without picking up minutenesses, which turn out so unreliable, let us at once ask the general question. There are three considerable bodies of Presbyterian Dissenters in Scotland—the Cameronians, the United Presbyterians, and the Free Church. Have the Cameronians become more or less narrow during their steadfast existence of nearly two centuries? Every one in Scotland knows the answer. Have the much larger body of United Presbyterians not got far more liberal and tolerant than they were at their outset? The affirmative is so signally true that it should not have been passed over in any estimate of Scotch ecclesiasticism. And, indeed, the recent history of this important body, compared with its contentions and splits

19

immediately after being severed from the Establishment, suggests in the strongest way the advantage, for the sake of liberality as of anything
else, of giving to Establishment and questions of
Establishment what sailors call a wide berth.
The greatest narrowness in Scotland has always
been on the rocks and shoals, either before or ·
immediately *after* the vessel has broken from the
beach, and while it is yet entangled with half-
secular questions of duty to the time. But take
even the Free Church, which has been only a
quarter of a century on the wave. Nothing is
clearer to any one who has watched it critically,
with a special eye to this very matter of liberality,
than that it has made steadfast progress year by
year since its birth ; and so certainly is this the
case, that a minority within it, which has a
political interest in being supposed to support
orthodoxy, is never weary of pointing out that
its liberality, growing for many years, amounts, in
their view, to a general and increasing laxity in
doctrine. The truth is, it is a very striking historical phenomenon how bodies like these should
have subsisted so long without any external tie
such as Establishment supplies, and should on the
whole have decidedly increased in liberality, while
never letting go the faith. And whatever may be

our judgment upon that relaxed hold of central truth which the Dean admires under the name of the Moderatism of last century, or upon the so-called Evangelical Revival in our own, the contrast between these strange alternations of sentiment within the Establishment, as compared with the steadfastness in doctrine and progress in liberality outside of it, should not have been omitted from any historical review.

I am puzzled by the first thing which Dean Stanley remarks of "the Scottish ecclesiastical struggles—that they are almost entirely of a negative character." No doubt, as the history went on, the Church bristled into all kinds of contentions and negations, applying its original principles to meet the difficulties and aggressions which surrounded it. But surely no one can read the history without seeing that the *chief* key to it must be the intensely positive and affirmative character of the belief originally taken up. The aspiration—

> " That the haill warld may see
> There's nane in the richt but we
> Of the auld Scottish nation ! "

—(though certainly not sung by the Covenanters at Dunse Law) may give the explanation of the

thing admirably, in so far as it was a characteristic of the national temper ; but deeper than even
the desire to subjugate others was the original conviction of having found "the right" in religious
matters.   "There is no other country in the
world," it is said, "that has what calls itself in so
many words a negative Confession."   Now, not to
say that one of the most important justifications
of Confessions has always been acknowledged to
be resistance to pressure from outside—not to
say, also, that the very name *negative* Confession,
applied to the Covenant of 1580, implies a reference to the fundamental Confession, framed by
Knox, which is throughout full of burning affirmation : to say nothing of all this, I challenge the
world to produce an example of a greater explosion
of positive conviction than is contained in the
head and front of this "negative" Confession
itself !   Read the very first sentence of it, and
cease to marvel that a nation which could utter
this with some good measure of honesty should
have its place in the world to fill :—

"We all and every one of us underwritten, protest,
That, after long and due examination of our own consciences in matters of true and false religion, we are
now thoroughly resolved in the truth by the Word
and Spirit of God ; and, therefore, we believe with

our hearts, confess with our mouths, subscribe with our hands, and constantly affirm, before God and the whole world, that this only is the true Christian faith and religion, pleasing God, and bringing salvation to man, which now is, by the mercy of God, revealed to the world by the preaching of the blessed evangel ; and is received, believed, and defended by many and sundry notable kirks and realms, but chiefly by the Kirk of Scotland, the King's Majesty, and the three estates of this realm, as God's eternal truth, and only ground of our salvation ! "

When the notable kirks and realms come once more in our day to feel the same hunger of the heart after the central truth, then they may be able rightly to judge of the history of Scotland. But, till then, they have nothing to draw with—and the well is deep.

Of course, even this massive block of affirmation —the corner-stone of all the Covenants—shows already in its rugged outlines the errors into which the Kirk was to fall. It was a noble Confession for a man freely to make; but it was a tyrannous test to impose on a family or people ! At least it became so when to this first utterance of common faith were added binding references to the details not only of Creed but of the manifold legislation with which Scotland had buttressed its Creed, and above all when the Creed of the Church,

freely uttered and liable to be freely changed on
further light as to the truth of God, was imposed
under penalties by the State. All through the
history of Scotland, there was no greater service
that could have been rendered to us by a distinguished stranger like Dean Stanley than to
point out how Scotland, holding the positive truth
firmly, might yet hold it freely—making a just
distinction between essentials and circumstantials,
or, at least, between more vital and less vital parts
of the organic truth—leaving room in the Church,
or in the Porch, for the youthful inquirer, the
ignorant inquirer, and the doubting inquirer—
and so cherishing the flame, without choking it,
as the heaven-sent lamp swings in the troubled
air. Scottish Presbyterianism has been gradually
feeling its way towards this in all its sections,
each touching the other, and gaining courageous
liberality from the contact ; but the essential condition of their attaining it has been that which
is dear to all of them, but which their mentor
earnestly repudiates, under the name of spiritual
independence—a name which, in Scotland, means
simply the catholic doctrine that the Church in
Church matters must obey God rather than man.
But even in this matter of its independence the
danger of the Kirk has always been to make it

rather a national than a catholic matter, to lay
too great stress on statutes recognising its rights
and establishment and giving it privileges, and
so to harass the consciences of others and weaken
its own. Hence Dr. Stanley finds it possible to
say that this "independence is as secular, as
political, as national, as ever. was the compliance
of the most latitudinarian of Erastians"—a great
mistake, contradicted by the documents of the
Kirk on all its great occasions, but countenanced
occasionally by ecclesiastical suicides, who find it
easier to rest on some political transaction, like
the Treaty of Union, than to adhere to anything
ike a principle.

But whatever difficulties Scotchmen may have
felt in adjusting this principle among themselves
in time past, they will be pretty nearly unanimous
when it is broadly impugned by one who is so
well entitled to represent Erastianism. And
Dr. Stanley has everywhere implied one thing
which has been hidden from many of his sym-
pathisers in Scotland, till his lectures have been
the means of bringing it out to all—that the
supremacy of the State *necessarily* means in the
long-run abnegation of absolute faith on the part
of the Church as a society. If all that is essential
to establishment is, as he lays it down, first,

"*some* religious expression of the community," no matter, seemingly, what external fact it bases itself upon ; and, secondly, that even this " religious expression be controlled and guided by the State,"[1] the State may, indeed, have a religious conscience, but the Church can have none. The Creed, to go no further, is in the hands of the State, not of the Church. And thus we come back at once to the relation of the Scotch Kirk to its Confessions—a matter which, on its own idea of spiritual independence, was perhaps not an easy thing to regulate; but if a trial, was a great and noble trial of living faith. For on the two principles of positive faith and freedom which the Scotch Church holds, it became not merely a natural but a necessary thing for it to repeat continually the great Protest prefixed by the pen of Knox to the Scottish Confession :—

" That if any man will note in our Confession any article or sentence repugning to God's Holy Word, that it would please him of his gentleness, and for Christian charity's sake, to admonish us of the same in write ; and we of our honours and fidelity do promise unto him satisfaction from the mouth of God, that is, from His Holy Scriptures, *or else reformation* of that which he shall prove to be amiss."

[1] *Essays on Church and State*, p. 347.

So, in 1647, the Kirk threw off the Confession of
Knox in a day, and re-formed its faith into another
symbol; and so day by day and year by year
it is its duty to make its Confession a true one,
holding to the faith, but binding upon its members
no more than they are bound to confess: a hard
duty, but a noble one, and one only compatible
with freedom. For, as we may now be allowed
formally to conclude, Establishment in Dr. Stanley's
s nse is demonstrably incompatible with independent belief in the Creed, on the part of a Church
which has given absolute power to the State
either to retain or alter it,—which has indeed
bound itself to teach the State's Creed.

But it will be said—though not in Scotland—
what matters it what the Church, as a body, does
as to Creed, provided individual ministers and
members take the enlightened course? And this
raises the matter of subscription—the proposed
treatment of which implied in every line of these
lectures fills me with absolute dismay, all the more
that there are so many influences tending to the
result. The Creed of all the Presbyterians of
Scotland, established and otherwise, is the same,
or nearly so; and they all bind their ministers
by subscription, though the Formula of the United
Presbyterian Church is the only rational and

Protestant one.[1]   But the non-established Presbyterian Churches all claim the right to vary
or abolish the existing Confession, and substitute
other utterances better expressing the Church's
faith, and also to vary or abolish the Formula.
In the Established Church the change can only
be effected by Parliament.   Now, I am not to
decide the question whether subscription should
exist at all.   There is a great deal to be said on
both sides of the question, and it should always
be in the Church's own hand to decide whether
it shall do so or not.   But there are infinitely
pathetic reasons why subscription, if it exists,
should be honest, and why no man should sign
a creed or formula which he does not believe.   It
is a subject on which no one can speak without
expressing his deep admiration of Dean Stanley's
exertions (whether we wholly agree with his
reasons or not) in the matter of the English
Church's subscription; and I cannot but regret
that on this question alone these most courteous
and kindly lectures on the sister Church should
faintly remind one of the maxim *Fiat experimentum
in*, etc.   For it is a ghastly experiment to make,

---

[1] "I acknowledge the Westminster Confession and
Catechisms as an exhibition of the sense in which I
understand the Holy Scriptures."

and one to save Scotland from which any sacrifice
is justifiable. And yet it is one which is imminent,
and which many, like the Dean of Westminster,
treat as inevitable. If you speak to a student
of the Free Church Divinity Halls about the
Confession of Faith, the chances are that he may
express uneasiness of conscience about the exact·
form of some minor things in it, and earnestly
desire that his sluggish Church leaders would strip
it of needless complexity ; but he is satisfied with
it as a whole—or if he is not, he slowly and sadly
retires (Scotland has many who have done so)
from the clerical profession. If in this year 1872
you speak to a student of the four Halls of the
Established Church on the same subject, it is quite
likely that you may find him in the most serious
state of discordance with the symbol of the Church's
faith ; but you do *not* necessarily find him raising
the question whether he ought to retire from his
profession.[1]   And yet both sign the same Formula,
" sincerely owning and believing the whole doctrine
contained in the Confession to be the truths of

---

[1] I retain this passage as it was written at the date
pointedly referred to ; but 1 should like to add that

1. While the public answer then given to it rather
suggested that I had stated the facts truly enough on
both sides, but had selected for praise the more pusil-
lanimous course, I received at the same time a private

God, and owning the same as the confession of
his faith." And the mass of the people to whom
the licentiate preaches accept these words in their
natural and plain significance. Whatever may be
done in England, the people of the North know
nothing about "Articles of Peace." Now, who
in this case will be forward to blame the sub-
scribing ministers? Certainly not those laymen
who, having themselves slipped their necks out
of God's collar, have no intention of ever signing
any Creed at all, but honour the high office which
they are unworthy to fill. We may not blame
individuals; but what a future for our country
if men are to commence systematically false subscription with a view to gradually relegating the
Confession to its place among historical monu-
ments! The price is too great to pay for *any*
result. It is no comfort to reflect that the same
mournful process has been going on in the past
in many a land before us. Think of the unspeak-
able laceration and abrasion of conscience that
must have occurred for generations in those

protest from a friend within the Edinburgh University
Divinity Hall assuring me that he knew the facts there
to be otherwise than I had put them; and

2. I am now inclined to think that while the twofold
general rule as to fact was roughly as I stated it, there
were more exceptions, on *both* sides, than I had supposed.

orthodox German States whose thrice-complicated
subscriptions Dean Stanley has recalled in his
paper on the subject. Think even of the "martyr
Renwick" taking his elders bound, when ordained
on the hillside, to stand by "all the lawful acts
of all the lawful General Assemblies of the true
Reformed Kirk of Scotland." What slow consuming ulcers have preyed on the hearts and
consciences of men of the finest nature when
standing between their oath on the one hand,
and the credulous people on the other! And are
we in Scotland on the verge of all this once more?
Far better by statute to abolish the Confession
of Faith altogether, or to strike asunder the bond
of subscription—far better do *anything*, than begin
again in the consciences of one-half the people
of Scotland that hideous process of mingled petri-
faction and decomposition !

For we have gone through it all already—we
remember the wormwood and the gall. I have
not space to refer in detail to the history of Creed
in Scotland in the last century, a most instructive
chapter which threatens to repeat itself in our
own. The Moderates—an evil race, Dr. Stanley's
elevation of whom as the model for the Kirk has
conclusively deprived his lectures of all dangerous
power in Scotland—had, in their time, the oppor-

tunity of dealing with this question of Creed; and
they did it characteristically. To quote Hugh
Miller, they, as a class, "robed themselves in the
habiliments of unbelief, but took the liberty of
lacing it with Bible edgings." Of course they
were not theoretical disbelievers in Christianity:
Warburton, when he said the Scotch clergy were
one half fanatics, and the other half infidels,
swung his mace with his usual reckless energy.
The unbelief was of the heart rather than of the
head. But it was prepared and entered upon
with very considerable deliberation. Early in the
century there was a great controversy on Creed,
in which the orthodox side was defended in the
mildest way, and as it died out the Moderates
seem to have resolved to leave things very much
as they were. They went on signing the Confession. They raised few controversies even about
details of it. But they began to treat the great
doctrines of it as things which it would be ridiculous for a gentleman and a scholar earnestly to
believe; and in their Creed, as in all Christian
Creeds, if the great doctrines are to be believed at
all, they can only be believed earnestly. And so
the thing went on, till, towards the close of the
century, a number of the clergy in the West,
having become distinctly Socinian, again raised

the question, and urged upon their leaders the
necessity of getting rid of a faith which all enlightened men throughout the Church had ceased
to believe. Principal Robertson retired rather
than consent to it; the French Revolution and
the new century came in, with its revival of
Evangelism, and ultimately an Evangelical majority, and with all the new responsibilities as to
the expression of the faith which devolve upon
men who believe it. The old bad time had passed;
but at what an expense! Take only one life
which the Moderates had cast away, that of Robert
Burns—"a pearl, richer than all their tribe." It
has recently been said that on them lies the responsibility that Burns, when he broke with the
orthodoxy of his time, did not seek something
better. I am thoroughly satisfied that this is
within the truth. An able writer[1] has recently
pointed out that the turning-point for evil in
Burns' life was his joining those clubs in Irvine
and Mauchline, which compounded for private
recklessness of life by flinging themselves into the
controversy raging at the time between the Ayrshire
Moderate ministers and the orthodoxy they had
sworn to and despised. But when it is suggested
that the poems of this date should be omitted

[1] In *Blackwood* for February 1872.

from all future editions as vulgar stuff, the answer
is, that it is impossible.   Leviathan is not so
tamed.   Such a ringing trumpet-call as—

> " Orthodox, orthodox, wha believe in John Knox,
>   Let me sound an alarm to your conscience,
> There's a heretic blast has been blawn in the West,
>   That *what is no sense must be nonsense* "—

can never, once written, be forgotten in Scotland,
though the " nonsense " in question may have been
the Divinity and Atonement of Christ.   But it
was not drunken writers and boozy lairds alone
who desired to seduce Burns into the Moderatism
which they could trust, as a religion that made
pleasant provision for the flesh.   There is an un-
speakably touching story handed down by tradition
in Ayrshire of Burns, when quite a young man,
having been visited, we know not how, by that
sudden consciousness of sin and despairing aspiration after a higher life which comes once in a lifetime to many a man.   He went, it is said, with
his " convictions " to the minister of the parish
where he happened to be—a Moderate of excellent
character—who heard all he had to say, and gave
it as his advice to him not to trouble himself about
these things—to " go to the first penny-wedding
he could find, and think no more about it."   I

have been unable to trace this story past the
general tradition, but the following I have from
the most eminent of modern Indian missionaries,
Dr. Duff, who heard it when on his missionary
tour in 1836 from an aged clergyman, in his youth
a contemporary of Burns. One of the leaders of
the Moderate party in Ayrshire having seen a
small manuscript collection of Burns' earliest poems,
sent for the poet. He treated him kindly and
praised his book; but pointing out passages here
and there which were tinged with the traditional
religion which the writer had imbibed under his
father's roof, advised him, for the sake of his own
future reputation, to avoid all drivelling pietism,
and keep henceforth such unpoetical stuff out of
his poems. Whether these incidents were before
or after the club-life and the first satirising of the
orthodox clergy I do not know; but assuming
that the latter were as narrow and bigoted and
bitter as Burns, poor fellow, describes them, it is
plain that the failure of his higher aspirations
were due not merely to that general atmosphere
of unbelief which his Moderate friends certainly
spread around him, but to their positive contact or
interference at the time when that glorious nature
was struggling to open itself to heaven. And so,
long after, when the weary life was drawing to a

20

close, and a stranger seeing Burns walking heavily into Dumfries took his arm to support him, and recognising the well-known face, broke out into affectionate religious talk, the world-worn poet is said, by what I believe is an undoubtedly true tradition, to have simply and kindly thanked him, adding that "there was a time when he might have taken an interest in these matters, but—he feared it was past now." A true man, almost always speaking the truth about himself, and worthy of having the truth spoken upon his tomb. But the truth about Burns, if it bears hard (as it does) upon even the faithful part of the Church in his day, can never be other than scathingly contemptuous of the Scottish Moderates.

And as they were in Ayrshire, so they were in Edinburgh. Dr. Stanley celebrates the friendly terms in which the leaders of the party lived with the chief theoretical opponents of Christianity.

" Hume was the great sceptic of a sceptical age. He was, however, of such a truly Christian character that such a good judge as Adam Smith said of him that he was the most perfectly wise and virtuous man he had ever known. Nor did Hume, like the scoffers on the Continent, ever put himself forward as an unbeliever. He said, 'I am no Deist : I do not so style myself ; neither do I desire to be known by that appellation.' His reward was that the graces of his character were acknowledged even more by the clergy than by the laity. . . . He lived on the most intimate terms with the leading clergy of Edinburgh. Blair openly defended him from attacks which he believed to be unjust. The General Assembly steadily refused, though hard pressed, to censure his writings."

It is all true, and it is not without its pleasing side. But was there any particular reason why the leading Moderates should *not* be friends with David Hume? He had six times their brains; his kindly good-nature passed with them and with Adam Smith for virtue; he was tolerant of themselves and seldom very contemptuous of the religion they professed; and if he made it a rule "never to put himself forward as an unbeliever," they were equally anxious never to put themselves forward as believers. It was all very natural; but I fail to see anything in it very meritorious or difficult of attainment. The cheapest of all virtues is tolerance on the part of men who have no faith; and to have no faith (in our nineteenth-century sense of earnest belief) was the very badge of the Scottish Moderate.

For, finally, I cannot but regard the Dean of Westminster's treatment of what called itself Moderatism in the Church of Scotland as alike misleading in history and mischievous in principle.

Historically, the name belongs exclusively to the
dominant party in the Church of Scotland in the
later part of the last and the beginning of this
century. It is permissible to point out analogies
between this party and others who lived before
or after them; but it is not a legitimate use of
history to include under a hitherto specially appro-
priated name men of the most diverse character
alike from those who bore it and from each other.
What authority is there for calling Carstairs, the
friend of William III., a Moderate? Still more,
what right can we possibly have to speak of Robert
Douglas as belonging to that class? We might
almost as well put MacCulloch of Cambuslang
among them. If the answer is that these were
men of moderation, it is true; but so, in the most
eminent degree, was Henderson, the Moderator of
the Assembly of 1638, and a far greater Presbyterian than either of them, and so, in an eminent
degree, was Welsh, who handed the Disruption
Protest to the Queen's Commissioner in 1843.
Moderation is a natural gift or a Christian grace
which individuals of all churches and parties
have shared; it is the monopoly of no nation or
sect, and it does not belong peculiarly to those
who value themselves exclusively upon it. On the
contrary, I do not hesitate to maintain that the

moderation of men of deep convictions, who happen
also to be wise and loving men, may, indeed, pass
by the same name as the moderation which in
others springs from want of convictions, but that
it is, seminally and essentially, a different quality,
and another thing. And so, when Scotchmen are
taught that "with the Revolution Settlement
begins the full ascendency of that great philosophic
virtue and evangelical grace in the Church of
Scotland, which has sometimes in these later days
been considered deadly heresy, but which the
Apostle commends to us as one of the most indis-
pensable of Christian duties—'Let your moderation be known unto all men'"—the question is
only raised whether the τὸ ἐπιεικές of the enthusiastic Apostle of the Gentiles and the moderation
of Blair were one thing; or whether rather they
were not two things in their inward nature so
irreconcilably opposed as to have little in common
but a word. But I must go further. To confound Moderatism with moderation appears a mis-
reading of history; but it is no less an error, I
suspect, to confound it even with Latitudinarianism;
as it certainly is, not to distinguish it from breadth.
All the Moderates were not Latitudinarians, nor
were all the Latitudinarians Moderates. The
Scottish Moderates, indeed, as a rule, clung to a

literal orthodoxy and to Presbytery, as they did to
their livings, and when they lapsed, lapsed into a
literal and narrow sort of Socinianism. They had
few tendencies to latitude; and, most certainly,
they had no breadth. Shallowness was their characteristic rather than breadth, and it was an
easier virtue to attain. They were no doubt largely
influenced by the great and learned men who
formed the Latitudinarian party in England; but
the influence, as it took effect on them, seems to
me to have been of a peculiarly unfortunate kind.
For Latitude is eminently an ambiguous virtue.
In one man it is a great and noble attainment; in
another it is the poor result of a poor nature; and
in all it is to be judged, not according to its degree,
but according to its kind. And as a transmitted
virtue it is received *in modum recipientis*. The
Moderates were men who had not got rid of doctrine, but who kept the doctrine and got rid of its
life; and it is only in a remote way that this can
be said to be derived from Tillotson and Chilling-
worth and the Latitudinarian school. But infinitely less can it be said to be derived from Baxter
and Leighton! These men, I take it, were not so
much Latitudinarians as men of breadth (and
the difference is often simply infinite); but their
latitude, like their moderation, was a whole pole

asunder from that of their supposed successors.
It is surely an astounding assertion that,

"however much in later days the Moderate party
in Scotland may have become 'of the earth, earthy,' it
was something for them to be able to claim as their
first founder the most apostolical and the most saint-
like of all Protestant Scotchmen."

There is no such genealogy—that which is born of
the flesh is flesh, and that which is born of the
spirit is spirit! Leighton had really no connection
with the Scottish Moderates, and Baxter had still
less. These two men were broad, and the Moderates were narrow; they loved peace, and the
Moderates loved sloth; they loved central truths
earnestly, and would therefore dispense with circumstantials, while the Moderates loved nothing
well enough to dispense with anything for the
sake of what they loved. An unlovely, cold-
blooded race! on their belly they must go, in
history, as in the century which they adorned.

Now, how is it that Dean Stanley, the quick-
eyed, sympathising friend of whatsoever things are
lovely and of good report through the wide realm
of history, has seemed to all Scotland to recommend
a gradual return to its condition in last century
as on the whole the best thing for the Scotch
Church? It is because his theory makes it a

necessity; because Erastianism (at least when
superinduced upon a Church that is free in the
utterance of its creed), requiring, as its condition,
a having-in-readiness to dispense with all Church
beliefs, requires also for its practical working that
the energy of Church life shall be lowered to
prepare for the inevitable conditions of the case.
And therefore it is that those Scotsmen who admire
him most personally, and are indeed under the
greatest obligations to his unfailing courtesy and
kindness, are yet unable to keep silence when the
question concerns the dearest interests of our
country. For it is a Scottish question. It would
be excessively rash to look with confidence for
equally disastrous results of Erastianism in England. We have had a very different history,
moving on a level of conscious Church life, from
which it is possible ruinously to fall. That this
Church life has in the past been too restricted, too
dogmatic, and too selfish, is certainly true. The
real heirlooms of the Presbyterianism of Scotland
have been its *depositum* of faith and its fiery
though contracted heart of love; but it has need
of the steadfast exertions of its sons in these days
to add to these the liberality and tolerance, " the
independence, the romance, the humour, the fervour,
the prudence," which, however insufficient as a

heritage in themselves, are precious as accessories and as aids. And in this direction it is making progress, though too timidly and slowly—too slowly, even though we grant that no permanent progress can be made *per saltum*, and that the first necessity for a country's future is not to break with its past. But while it would be unwise to break suddenly with the past, even in matters of indifference and detail, it would be ruin to break with its whole vital principle in the way that is now proposed. It is not merely that Scotsmen have a pathetic and patriotic interest in the kirk and creed of their fathers; that—

> " The souls of now three hundred years
> Have laid up here their hopes and fears
> And all the treasure of their pain—
> Ah! yet consider it again."

We are bound to consider it under a sense of responsibility to the present; for as a nation judges its history, it is itself being judged. And the great law, for a man or a people, is, " *We needs must love the highest when we see it, not Lancelot, nor another.*" The dashing, romantic, Scottish Episcopalian type of Walter Scott has been our Lancelot, flushed with the light from the "low sun" of departing chivalry; and it will not be forgotten. But we have had a higher and graver

call, and, with many faults of self-conceit and
hardness and narrowness, have yet as a nation
hearkened to it.   No doubt we need catholicity,
elasticity, variety, and sympathetic adaptation;
but there are more ways than one in which a
nation may seek these gifts.   The one way is very
easy, and very worthless; the other, that which
retains ardent religious conviction and strives to
add to it toleration, is very hard and high.   But
it is the only way in which it is fit that Scotland
should walk, or in which it is desirable to succeed.

THE LAST TWENTY YEARS.

IT is in dealing with contemporary matters especially that the eye sees what it is capable of
seeing. There are those who look out on the
great age in which we live, and from Dan to
Beersheba find it barren. But how can the world
be other than barren to men who seek small
things, and seeking find them? To such an un-
generous temper little that is noble in human
life reveals itself. Even in the past it is the
noisier events—the drums and tramplings of
history—that fill their unbelieving ears. But
the surest punishment of such observers is the
incapacity to understand their own age. Contemporary history inevitably becomes to them
a game of shifting expedients and personal
intrigue; and mankind, even when wrestling
with the larger problems of existence, seem but
an ignoble crowd, struggling along the narrower
ways of life " with too much envy in their hearts
and too much striving in their hands."

There have been ages and there have been countries where there was some excuse even for such distortion. There have been times when the public relations of human life were cast in so poor a mould, and when that mould had become so hardened around whole generations, that the only deliverance for individual thinkers and Christians was in casting their eyes back into some earlier and golden age, or in stretching onward beyond the encompassing facts of history to the ideals of faith. God be thanked! the lot of men in our day —of men in Scotland at least—is not so hard. There, no doubt, as elsewhere, the great battle is within, and these essays do not deal with the deepest strivings. Yet even to these—to individual aspiration and inward progress—the barriers interposed from without are fewer in our time than they ever were before. And in the matters of organisation and association which are here discussed (because in them inward and individual principles must find fit scope, if not embodiment), our case is better still. We have no longer to flee from encompassing facts to distant ideals. On the contrary, our ideals stand without upon the threshold, and press at a half-opened door.

It is so in the matter of Creed, the history of which for the last quarter of a century has

already been resumed. During that period Presbyterianism in Scotland has realised its unity with
Presbyterianism everywhere else, and it has found
the world-wide system not locked or blocked, but
everywhere moving, and moving on its proper axis.
Its freedom to vary or remodel the Puritan Creed
extends to going back to the earlier Reformation
models, but is by no means limited even by these.
The Reformed Church in Scotland has never
abandoned its inheritance in the great Creeds
of the Christian East, and the free use of these
(as distinguished from the *damnosa hereditas* of
an ecclesiastical or civil obligation to use them)
is the right alike of scholarship and of faith, and
may play a considerable part in the future. So
long, indeed, as other powerful churches are not
only themselves bound by these symbols, but make
them a link in the chain by which the sacerdotal
past would bind the present, a democratic church
in Scotland is likely to use them only in its theological schools. For external freedom is essential
to our ideal in this matter. Of course the freedom
must be more than external. In the membership
of all our churches there is much creed-making in
the sense of new-moulding of individual faith, and
one of the great questions of the day is how far
that can be represented in the new-moulded theo-

logy. And when that theology has come into existence, and has adjusted its relations with the old, the question may follow, how far it too will demand the acceptance of new language and of its own forms. But even that question, when it comes, if it comes, will not bring the Presbyterian ideal nearer us than at this moment it is. The faith of private members of that communion has long been practically free from the fetters alike of the ancient documents which bind men outside it, and of the modern documents which for genera-tions it was attempted rigidly to impose. The question of revision is now really raised by the varying subscriptions which each church may consider appropriate to the various grades of its officials. Here also much mischief may no doubt be done; in the ordinary case by slothful cruelty, and occasionally by precipitate experiment. But the Boards of Revision, sitting more or less permanently on both sides of the Atlantic, give us more than an occasional and constitutional relief in cases where the tension has become too great. Even when they do not for the moment effect much, the great principle of legitimate free-dom which they embody—a principle which in the recollection of men still living had almost passed into oblivion—is found to be, in its mere exhibition, at once a tonic to conscience and a balm to faith. And it opens a clear future—a future which is likely to be unembarrassed until Anglo-Catholicism rouses itself to put to our free churches the question, whether after all it is necessary to stand fast in this particular liberty with which in the present generation they have been set free.

But the twenty years have resulted for Scotland in the culmination of the more general question of combined civil and religious liberty. They were ushered in by an advance in this matter of the greatest importance, even on the European scale. Rome, in the Syllabus of 1864 and the Council of 1870, had renewed the claim of the church to be established, and that in the modern state. France, since 1830, and Germany, since 1848, had already rejected that claim, and they were now joined by Austro-Hungary. From the Atlantic to the border of Russia "full and entire liberty of religion and of conscience" was proclaimed as the basis of the European constitutions, and all citizens, no matter what their religious profession or lack of it, were declared to have equal rights before the law. In Scotland the same question was stirred at the same time by the proposal, enthusiastically received, to confer religious equality upon Ireland.

21

But the convictions, suddenly appealed to by these events from without, had been here long and slowly forming in the consciences of men.

To the United Presbyterian Church must always pertain the honour of being the first in Scotland to maintain the principle, not of Church freedom only, but, in connection with it, of civil liberty and religious equality before the law. It is a great mistake to suppose that their strenuous argument for these combined principles, which had so great an effect on the masses of the people about the time of the Reform Bill of 1832, did not tell also on the members and the leaders of the Scottish Established Church. A writer of authority in the Free Church has recently brought out [1] how this pressure from without was very much the origin of the determination on the part of the Church of Scotland and its most eminent champions —of Dr. Chalmers in particular—to assert that independence of the State which they found (as the Dissenters forewarned them they would) to be practically inconsistent with Establishment. But to rise higher still, and demonstrate that religious liberty must be based on civil liberty,

[1] See the Sixth Lecture in *Church and State in Scotland* (Chalmers Lectures), by Thomas Brown, D.D., Edinburgh, 1892.

and that civil liberty means religious equality before the law, was the special attainment of the Scottish Dissenters of the early century. Outside our island that principle (with certain variations, which are not improvements, in its continental working) has become a basis of Western civilisation on both sides of the Atlantic. Borrowed by American legislation from our own older thinkers, and borrowed by the constitutions of Western Europe from America, it came back to our shores with the Reform movement of 1830. And in Scotland it was maintained with conclusive force of argument, not in the public press only (and the public press did not then shrink from urging electors to take their convictions to the poll), but on the religious platform too. The genius and enthusiasm of the rising leaders within the Church did indeed prevail to suggest an experiment once more, whether after all such a body could be maintained and extended by the State, and yet remain free. The experiment was tried. But in the meantime the arguments of the Scottish Voluntaries roused the conscience of the people on the side of civil justice, even more than they had touched that of members of the Establishment on the side of the freedom of their Church. And the result has been that in the revived discussions incessantly carried on during the last fifteen years, and eminently during the last two, no attempt has been made to meet this central argument of justice. Alike in meetings of voters and constituents and in gatherings of representative delegates, no matter to what Presbyterian Church the majority present may have belonged, the argument from civil equity, whenever advanced, has almost always been unanswered, and has always been victorious; while in mere Church Defence meetings it has been eloquently ignored. And no wonder. There are not ten Presbyterians in Scotland who will admit, that if Scotland showed a clear majority of, say, Unitarians or Episcopalians, that would justify the State in compelling themselves and the other members of the minority to support a Unitarian or Episcopalian Church. There are no doubt more than ten who would hold precisely the same compulsion justified when it happens to be exercised in their own favour. But the protest of conscience lies very near the surface in all such cases. And when it is remembered that Establishment, as it at present exists in Scotland, excludes half the Presbyterians as well as all other Christians, it may be safely said that, making the usual allowance for the inevitable moral lunatic, all thinking men there are satisfied that it is in its working unjust, and that the present state of matters should in some way be terminated.

Even the question on what plea this obligation may be best avoided or postponed divides men more equally than is imagined. You must find some defensive plea either in the future or in the past. I pass by the mere cynicism which confines itself to the immediate future, in the hope that some accident—say, a particular election—may change the present establishment minority in Scotland into a working majority. That of course would not meet the moral question; it would only raise it. It would not entitle, it would only enable, a majority to do wrong. It would empower them to do to others the kind of wrong which at present is done to themselves by others.[1] But the real hope for the future is that the State shall either terminate, or seem to terminate, the wrong; by broadening that relation to its citizens which is at present so exclusive, and therefore so unjust. And this may be done in more ways than one. At the present moment the idea of widening the Scottish ecclesiastical body, so as to make it a "clerisy" or Church of culture, rather than a

---

[1] Practically by England, whose Parliamentary representatives now override ours in our Church matters, as they did memorably on March 7th, 1843.

Church of Christ, has fallen into the background. But it is sure to re-emerge, probably in the first place in connection with the long-continued scandal of our sectarian Universities. And the plan of levelling up the emoluments of all religious bodies is as certain to be discussed as that of levelling down the doctrine of one. It must not be forgotten that the principle of Religious Equality, accepted as fundamental on the Continent, may be carried out thoroughly, if not wisely, by the method of concurrent endowment adopted in France. There every denomination, Christian or otherwise, which can show a hundred thousand adherents, is admitted to share, according to its numbers, in the State subsidy ; while the Catholic Church, acknowledged in the Bourbon Charter as " the Church of the State," has since its rejection in 1830 been only that of "the majority of Frenchmen." This of course is parting with the old theory on which the State action was a homage to truth. But it conforms to the new or constitutional theory, which makes its action a homage to justice. When such plans are proposed or suggested in Scotland, as they no doubt will be, it should be remembered that the test of their honesty will be the willingness to take the first step of doing right, by giving up the establishment of the body to be no longer exceptionally favoured. There is always a tendency, however, when ascendency or preference can no further be maintained on theory, to prolong it on the ground of simple selfishness; and the compromises proposed in such cases are peculiarly demoralising, chiefly, I think, because they are unconscious defences against the new ideals which have been pressing on the consciences concerned. In Scotland there is but one step—a very short and simple one—between us and the ideal of absolute civil justice in Church matters. And the same short step would open before us that other ideal or " imagination " of Church union which shone before the eyes of our fathers, undarkened now by the civil compulsion in which their grim theory of State duty framed it.

For the last few years, indeed, the avoidance of the one step into simple justice has been based not so much on the future and its plans, as on the past and its traditions. It is admitted that the present state of matters is unjust or exclusive, and should in some way be terminated. But it is constantly suggested that our original Scottish Establishment, or at least its theory or ideal, was not so partial or unjust, and that it may therefore be permanently or provisionally adhered to. Of

328 STUDIES IN SCOTTISH HISTORY.

course this is exactly the converse of the truth.
The principle of establishment by the mere power
of a majority is obviously, we may almost say
admittedly, unjust. But the principle on which
establishment in Scotland—and everywhere else in
Europe—was historically founded is a great deal
more so. For it was the principle of sheer intolerance—the magistrate being held bound to compel
every citizen to be personally a member and a
worshipper in the one church, and of course (as
a very subordinate corollary) to contribute to its
maintenance. Now to the maintenance of *a*
church we are still forced to contribute, but it is
no longer the church in which we are, as subjects,
bound to be all of us members and worshippers.
That the principle[1] upon which Parliament sup-

---

[1] Half of the fact upon this matter has been well
stated, alike at the opening and at the close of the twenty
years, by the foremost opponent of Religious Equality
in Scotland. "There can be no doubt whatever that
Established Churches cannot be extended in our times
upon the same principles on which they were founded.
In fact, I believe that the circumstances of society and
the position of the Christian Church, which enabled
Established Churches to be founded for the first time, are
no longer existing anywhere in Europe." Not only so, but
"If it were now possible to secure the extension of the
Established Churches by Parliamentary grants, I am
prepared to contend that this would not really be an

ports a privileged sect in the present day is not really
"the same as that on which the Established Church
was originally founded," has been almost admitted,
and is quite true. (It cuts in two, however, the
whole equivoque of defence sometimes drawn from
that origin, and in particular from the ancient
statutes, which all rest on the old idea, not on the ·
new.)[1] Which of the two principles—the old prin-

extension of the same principle as that on which Established Churches were originally founded." (Speech by
the Duke of Argyll at Helensburgh, on the 1st of October,
1873.) And what was the doctrine of the civil magistrate
upon which that establishment and that endowment were
originally founded? "There was one error into which our
Reformers fell, and unless we remember that error, we
shall never fully understand their position. They therefore—it was very wrong in them, for it was against
some of their own principles—applied to Parliament,
not merely to sanction their Confessions of Faith, but
to insist upon all men believing them; and they laid
down a doctrine as to the power of the civil magistrate,
which it is impossible for us to understand until we
remember the point of view from which they worked,
which was, that all the laity of the country were the
laity of one church." (Speech at Edinburgh, January
13th, 1892.)
  [1] So true is this, that our ablest theological teachers,
Presbyterian and otherwise, are at this moment excluded
from the chairs in the four Scottish Universities, not by
any statute in favour of one body above another, but by
an old Act which forbids all, not being members of the

ciple of intolerance, which kept every citizen
within the one church, or the new principle of
partiality, which keeps the hand of one citizen in
the pocket of his unoffending neighbour—which of
these two is the more odious, may not be easy to say.
But it is very easy to say which is more remote
from any ideal. The old European principle,
which makes even the State the pillar and ground
of religious truth, had a certain deceived greatness.
Our modern insular practice, severed from that
past ideal by an impassable gulf, severs itself in
procrastinating timidity from the twofold ideal of
the future—the obligation of the State to the
highest justice, and the obligation of the Church
to the highest truth.

But during those twenty years there was another
object perhaps more influential than even that
of religious justice. It was that of Church
Union. The obvious reasonableness of this hope
struck all observers; not those within only,
but at least equally those without or above.
" Thank God ! " writes the Queen in her Diary
on October 3rd, 1869—" Thank God ! there is no

Church Established, to teach youth any step of learning
from spelling to theology, no matter whether the teaching
be within or without the Universities, or even in a private
and adventure school.

difference of form or doctrine here, and were this [disestablishment in Scotland] to happen, the Free Church and the United Presbyterians, with the present Established Church, would become one very strong Protestant body." But with Scottish Presbyterians the matter was of course one not of observation and probability, but of historical obligation and religious principle. For some years before the royal anticipations were thus recorded, the duty of Church reconstruction had already been the main subject of interest and study of the two churches first named, in their union negotiations. One of them, the United Presbyterian Church, had been itself the result and aggregate of a very remarkable series of unions and reunions. And all of these were founded on the Old Seceder passion for Presbyterian union.[1] The origin of the Free Church, on the other hand, as previous chapters have reminded the reader, was such as to make union, on a national scale, a central object of ambition. Consequently, when the negotiations closed in 1873, resulting only in a

[1] A Scottish judge once threw out the view that an obligation to unite with other Presbyterians would have been " a very strange condition " of trust for a congregation of Old Seceders. Nothing could show a more complete ignorance of the whole literature and spirit of the religionists dealt with.

scheme of "Mutual Eligibility" of ministers of
the two churches, that was, in the view of both,
only a first step towards a future amalgamation,
and, in the view of some of their members, towards
a still larger union.

The question of union, however, now received
even more prominence on the side of the Church
Established, and in connection with the abolition
of lay patronage. The special object of that movement had been stated, as early as June 18th, 1869,
by the Church of Scotland deputation to Mr.
Gladstone as Prime Minister, to have been "the
conciliation of the Free Church"; and although
this was subsequently disclaimed in Parliament
for purposes of debate, it was largely true, and
was highly honourable to all concerned. Unfortunately the proposal to express this feeling, and
to acknowledge the interest in the matter of the
Presbyterians outside in a formal statement on
the subject to be issued by the Church, was opposed
and overruled. The result was, that when the
Act was passed in 1874, what ought to have been
an opportunity for approximation, became rather
a cause of controversy. The eccentric suggestion
that the Free Church separation from the State
of the year 1843 was due to Patronage was met
by a declaration of the Free Church Assembly, that

the abolition of Patronage, which it highly approved, did not even "affect" the grounds of that separation. Men so cautious as the late Sir Henry Moncrieff now took an active part in tabling the affirmation that the divisions of Scotland were to be healed by nothing short of a termination of the existing connection between the Church and the State in Scotland. And all this discussion of fairness and equity as between churches blended itself, in the minds of electors voting under a now extended franchise, with a sense of civil justice and the abhorrence of religious privilege.

Consequently when Lord Hartington came down to Scotland in 1877 as, during Mr. Gladstone's retirement, the leader of the Liberal party, he was able to describe the Patronage Abolition Act of 1874 as "a step in the direction towards Disestablishment," and to pledge English Liberals to accept, on the latter question, the conclusions for Scotland of the Liberalism of Scotland, without reference to the separate interests of England and of the church established there. "All I can say is, that when, if ever, Scotch opinion, or even Scotch Liberal opinion, is fully formed upon this subject, I think that I may venture to say on behalf of the Party as a whole that it will be prepared to deal with the question on its merits,

and without reference to any other consideration." [1]
Mr. Gladstone's acceptance of this pledge in a
striking speech next year in Parliament [2] was
made more important by his arranging with both
sides, [3] when coming forward as candidate for
Midlothian, under what conditions this reference
to Scotland should be carried out. His early in-
timation, that the question was already tabled in
Scotland for an "intelligible and distinct" answer,
and was not to be postponed till some perhaps
impossible isolation at a future election, was at
once noted and acted upon by both parties, with
a view to the question having a "fair, full, and
open trial." The trial, however, was, as Mr.
Gladstone had carefully pointed out, not whether
one church was doing church work as meritoriously
as the others, but whether it could "show that
the exclusive enjoyment of the national property
which has been set apart for ecclesiastical purposes

[1] Speech at Edinburgh, November 6th, 1877.

[2] June 18th, 1878.

[3] In letter of May 24th, 1879 (*Times*, June 24th),
written, with concurrence of Lord Hartington, in answer
to Memorial from Liberal Churchmen desiring that the
question of Disestablishment should not be raised, till it
could be presented as a main issue not mixed up with
others, and to a counter-demand, through Principal Rainy,
that the question should be held open even to the Parliament of 1880.

in Scotland, by one religious communion," ought
to be maintained. And the result has been that
during the last twelve years an incessant education
of the Scottish people in this great question has
gone on in each parish and constituency, and
during every month of every year, but culminating
of course increasingly during each of the three
General Elections which have already passed.
The years 1882 and 1883 were specially distinguished by the progress made through discussions
on public platforms; the members of the Free
Church, as the intermediate Church body, being
then specially appealed to. The local Liberal
Associations, however, were also steadily discussing,
and one by one making up their minds on the
matter; and in view of the pledge by Mr. Gladstone and Lord Hartington to Scottish Liberalism,
the answer which its undivided representatives
gave—before any division was introduced by the
Irish question—is of historical interest. In September 1885 the Liberal delegates, called to meet
Mr. Chamberlain from all the counties and burghs
of Scotland, pronounced by ten to one in favour
of Liberal Equality and Disestablishment; and
next month the official Liberal Association itself,
representing the slower political temperament,
resolved, by a vote of four hundred delegates to

seven, that "the time is now come for making Disestablishment a plank of the platform of Scottish Liberalism." Of course these numbers did not represent the exact proportions of the rank and file of Liberalism who had in 1885 attained to definite convictions on this matter. They showed, however, the overpowering drift of opinion among the representatives who in each district had the responsibility of voting upon a question which was pressed upon them all, partly by their own sense of justice, and partly by the Liberal leader and his two rather contrasted lieutenants. And it was not till years after this, on May 2nd, 1890, that Mr. Gladstone followed the majority of Scottish members in the vote so long anticipated.

For the last fifteen years, if not fifty, the matter had thus become unmistakably practical politics. It does not follow that it had lost its place among the duties of churches. Whenever, during that time, the question of justice pressed upon the conscience of an unwilling churchman, he invariably alleged that it was a matter for politicians. But whenever, during the same time, the political duty was urged upon an unwilling elector, his inevitable answer was that it was an affair for the Church. Current literature, indeed, shows, in a most curious way, that the two excuses were tendered in a numerically equal proportion. But as the years went on it was clear that the work of Church inquiry had begun earlier, and was more exhaustively done. On the side of the Established Church, indeed, the recent manifestoes have been confined to eloquent but general defence, or to kindly but general invitation. But at an earlier date the proposals of the Patronage Act and of a Bill by Mr. Finlay gave opportunity for more definite discussion. Yet even then the absence of any answer to the Free Church protest of 1843, and of any authoritative document which might take its place, left great doubt as to the attitude of the Church to its legal obligations laid down at that date. It is impossible, even for those who have given the keenest attention to the matter for many years, to predict whether that Assembly would agree with its distinguished representatives, who urge that since 1874 their Church must be held to have gone over to the side it rejected in 1843, or with the less known but consistent controversialists, who still attack the Claim of Right.[1] There is much more certainty as to the

---

[1] See p. 135 as to the former. On the latter side there is the recent republication of a paper by the keen but courteous writer we have recently lost, whom I knew and respected as *Veritas*.

22

attitude which the people outside of Assemblies would take to the complex question of Church freedom, Church union, and religious equality. Of course during all those years the conferences upon the matter between members of the churches have been incessant, and sometimes very influential. But there has been none between the Churches as such. In 1886, the Free Church, approached most courteously by the Church of Scotland as to union, offered to go into conference on that subject on the footing of making Disestablishment and Disendowment—though it had repeatedly affirmed both—open questions in the discussion, if the other conferring body would do the same. But the offer was declined, and the question passed into the hands of the responsible electorate.

And this is what is called Church History in Scotland !

Not so. The true Church History, in Scottish theory, is quite another thing. Whenever, during these last twenty years, in crowded city or on distant moor, a young man, smitten with a sudden remembrance of God, has turned a shame-filled face to Him who has still power on earth to forgive sins, and has set up His worship, not in chapel or cathedral, but as priest over his own family and home, there, as our fathers have taught us, is already begun the real history of the true Church. And wherever such a man has been found, among his fellows abroad or within his house at home, going his way with a pure plain heart, and seeking the good of others rather than his own, there already that history has attained its fragrance and flower. Many of the things, indeed, towards which Scottish faith and feeling are now most strongly drawn, are in no respects ecclesiastical, or connected with the Church as a corporate body. And even when that faith and feeling prompt, as in the future they no doubt will, to action and sacrifice on a larger scale, both the action and the sacrifice may find their place among the civic and secular, rather than the Church relations of men—of men stimulated from within, no doubt, but stimulated to work along with all their fellow-citizens outside.

Yet even to works external to the church, its members must go with clean hands. It is sometimes said that the State relations of the Church in Scotland, always foreign to its proper life, have in modern times very little to do with our practical religious work, and need not be much complained of. Yet they are found now, as much as in any age of the past, to irritate the conscience which is

sensitive to injustice. A grain of sand is not in
itself of importance. But a grain of sand in the
eye is of importance—until it is removed. And
after all we cannot forget the hope towards which
with us the cleansed eye strains. Private piety,
when it works with as well as for others, becomes
in Scotland public patriotism in the Church,
and has to gird itself to do the work of its
time. And that work may often be, as now, a
work of construction or reconstruction. Of such
construction the first necessity is, that we build
upon no one stone which is stained and flawed
with deliberate wrong; and that when bribed—
even with money that should be our own—to do to
others, by a majority, what we should count it
unjustice for others, by a majority, to do to us, we
shall refuse. But behind these plainer precepts,
and in order to do the work of the time intelli-
gently and consistently, more may be desirable.
There is no class of the Scottish people really
inclined to injustice or to sectarianism, and their
difficulties in Church matters, like their hopes, are
founded on a long and complicated history in the
past. It is a legitimate attempt to review that
past, with the object of disentangling from among
the conflicting opinions of our fathers the true
root principles, which held them, and to which we

must hold. For principles are not things in themselves inconsistent; and history is not a rope of sand; and wisdom will in due time be justified, even of those who are not her children.

FINIS.

Printed by Hazell, Watson, & Viney, Ld., London and Aylesbury.